THE GIANT DINOSAUR BOOK

KINGfISHER
NEW YORK

Acknowledgments

The publishers wish to thank the following for supplying photographs for this book:

Page 8 U.S. Dept. of Interior; 9 Imitor; 10 Illustrated London News; 11 Imitor (top), Michael Benton (bottom); 12 Zophia Kielan-Jaworowska; 13 Zophia Kielan-Jaworowska (right), Michael Benton (left); 15 Dinosaur National Museum (top), Michael Benton (bottom); 16 Levi-Setti, Enrico Fermi Institute; 18 Michael Chinery; 19 Natural History Museum; 20 Bruce Coleman; 21 Pat Morris; 23 Michael Chinery; 26 Bruce Coleman; 29 Pat Morris; 31 Biofotos; 39 ZEFA; 42 Imitor; 43 Pat Amos; 45 Imitor; 46 Zophia Kielan-Jaworowska; 57 National Geographic/James Amos; 61 Natural History Museum; 63 Bruce Coleman; 65 Imitor; 68 Pat Morris; 70 Museum of Natural History, Berlin; 73 Imitor; 75 Imitor; 77 Peabody Museum (left), ZEFA (right); 80 Solarfilma; 81 U.S. Natural History Museum.

Picture Researcher: Elaine Willis

Author David Lambert
Consultant Dr. Michael Benton
Edited by Sian Hardy
Designed by Michèle Arron
Cover design by Mike Davis
Illustrators include Jeremy Gower, George Thompson,
Kevin Maddison, Alan Male, Jim Channell

Kingfisher
Larousse Kingfisher Chambers Inc.
80 Maiden Lane
New York, New York 10038
www.kingfisherpub.com

First published as *The Illustrated Book of Dinosaurs* by Kingfisher Publications Plc 1991
This edition printed in 2001
2 4 6 8 10 9 7 5 3 1
1TR/0701/TIM/--[RNB]/140MA

LIBRARY OF CONGRESS CATALOGING-IN-PUBLICATION DATA
has been applied for.

ISBN 0-7534-5421-1

Printed in China

contents

giants of the past

Dinosaurs died out millions of years ago, but these prehistoric creatures still fascinate us today. No wonder, for they were masters of the land some 75 times longer than humans have been living on the earth.

Dinosaur discovery started in the 1820s, when scientists began to realize that the huge fossil bones they found in ancient rocks belonged to prehistoric creatures unlike anything now alive. Bit by bit, anatomists pieced the bones together to rebuild skeletons. From these they tried to work out the animals' shapes and sizes, as well as how they stood, walked, fed, and fought. Because so much was guesswork, they made many mistakes. Skulls were sometimes placed at the tip of a tail and a spiked thumb was once mistaken for a horn!

Since those first discoveries, scientists who probe the past have learned a great deal more about the dinosaurs. We now know that the early dinosaurs and their ancestors were lively, long-legged, hunting reptiles, not much bigger than a rabbit. True dinosaurs appeared about 230 million years ago. Over time, they spread to all the continents, which were then joined together to form one huge supercontinent.

Different kinds of dinosaurs developed. From the first two-legged meat-eaters came many more. The smallest grew no bigger than a cat; the largest weighed as much as an elephant. Such predators were the biggest hunting animals that ever lived on land.

▼ *These eight dinosaurs include four plant-eaters and four flesh-eaters.* Brachiosaurus *browsed among the treetops while* Triceratops, Edmontosaurus, *and* Stegosaurus *cropped leaves nearer the ground with their horny beaks.* Compsognathus *and* Ornitholestes *were small hunting dinosaurs that chased lizards through the undergrowth.* Deinonychus *may have killed medium-sized plant-eating dinosaurs by slashing at them with its claws.* Tyrannosaurus *probably charged big dinosaurs head first, taking great chunks of flesh out of their sides with its huge jaws.*

These monsters preyed on plant-eating dinosaurs. They too branched out into many kinds. Small, two-legged plant-eaters gave rise to much larger animals. Most of these walked on all fours. Plant-eaters built like monstrous giraffes included the longest and heaviest land animals of all time. Between them, hunting and plant-eating dinosaurs filled the places taken today by mammals such as lions and cheetahs, deer, antelopes, giraffes and elephants.

By 1990, scientists had named hundreds of different kinds of dinosaur. Many of these have been named since 1970 and new discoveries are made every year. As each new discovery is made, scientists change their ideas about what the dinosaurs were like. People used to think of dinosaurs as cold-blooded animals. These need the Sun's heat to make them warm enough to move around. Today, many scientists believe that dinosaurs' bodies were always warm, much as mammals' bodies are. People once thought of dinosaurs as slow plodders. Scientists now believe that some could run as fast as a horse. Because most dinosaurs had tiny brains, people used to think they were stupid. Now we know that many were quite crafty creatures and that some led fairly complex lives.

Then, about 65 million years ago, the dinosaurs died out. Their sudden disappearance is just one of the many mysteries that scientists still puzzle over today.

In the pages that follow, we shall trace the story of the dinosaurs. You will find some words are in **bold** type. This means that they are explained further in the Glossary.

the fossil hunters

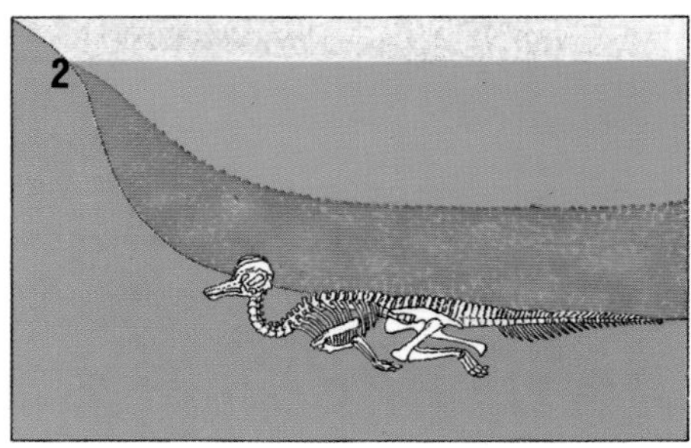

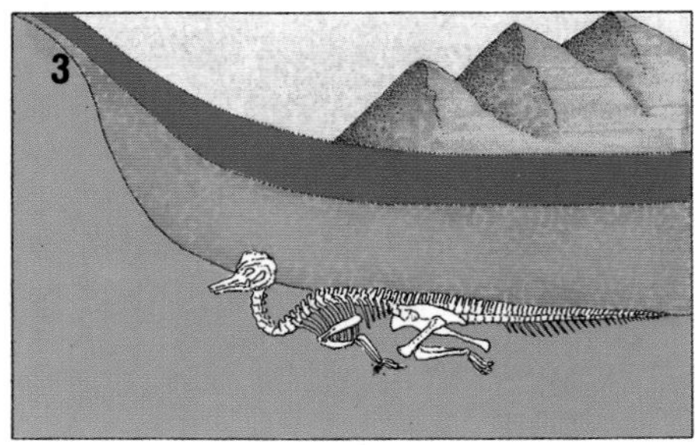

▲ *This dead dinosaur (1) is a fossil in the making. Its body is washed away by the river and settles on the river bed. There its soft parts rot away, leaving only the hard skeleton. This is covered by layers of mud and, in time, minerals replace the bone (2). As more layers build up, the pressure gradually turns the bones into rock. They have become fossils (3). Much later, earth movements push the fossil up to the surface, where it is uncovered by the action of wind and rain (4).*

Most of what we know about the dinosaurs comes from bones and tracks that have been preserved as **fossils** in rocks. The Ancient Greeks noticed fossil animals more than 2,400 years ago. But no one knew for sure how fossils were formed. By about 400 years ago, scientifically minded people realized that fossil seashells had once belonged to creatures living in the sea. Somehow the shells had become stuck in rocks on land, even high up on mountains. But how? One popular explanation was that a great flood had once drowned the world then left the shells high and dry. How fossils were really formed remained a mystery until about 200 years ago.

How fossils really formed

We now know that most fossil dinosaurs are the remains of corpses that fell in rivers, lakes, or seas and settled on the mud or sand below. The dead dinosaurs' soft parts soon rotted away, but their hard bones and teeth were covered by layers of mud or sand. This saved them from decay. In time, thick layers of mud or sand built up, squashing the layers beneath. These slowly hardened into limestone, sandstone, and other layered, or **sedimentary**, rocks. Water carrying dissolved minerals down through the rocks filled tiny holes in the buried dinosaur bones. The minerals strengthened the bones against the pressure of the rocks above and the bones were preserved as fossils. Dinosaur teeth, however, were so hard that many

have survived almost unchanged. Sometimes, a bone dissolved away and left a bone-shaped hole. This is called a mold. If minerals filled the hole, they formed a fossil called a cast. Molds and casts are very rare, however.

After millions of years, earthquakes thrust some fossil-bearing rocks above the sea. Rain, wind, and frost gnawed away parts of the rocks and the fossil dinosaurs were left exposed. Of the millions of dinosaurs that once walked the earth, however, very few ever became fossils. Even fewer will show up on the surface and be found.

The hunt begins

As long ago as 1677, Dr. Robert Plot, a professor at Oxford University in England, described a dinosaur thigh bone that he had found. Dr. Plot thought the huge bone came from a giant man. It wasn't until the 1820s that people realized that these bones belonged to huge animals that no longer existed.

The first dinosaur discoveries were made in England. In 1824, Professor William Buckland of Oxford University described strange, ancient bones that had been dug up near Oxford. Among them was a large jawbone with teeth like knives. Buckland called its prehistoric owner *Megalosaurus* ("giant reptile"). *Megalosaurus* was the first dinosaur to get a proper, scientific name.

At about the same time, Mary Mantell, a doctor's wife, noticed some fossil teeth lying in a pile of roadmenders' stones. She collected them for her husband, who was a keen fossil hunter. Dr. Mantell realized that the teeth must have belonged to an unknown, giant, prehistoric creature. In 1825, he named it *Iguanodon* ("iguana tooth"), because its teeth reminded him of an iguana lizard's teeth.

Over the next few years, workmen unearthed more fossil teeth and bones in southern England. The leading anatomist of the time, Sir Richard Owen, concluded that they belonged

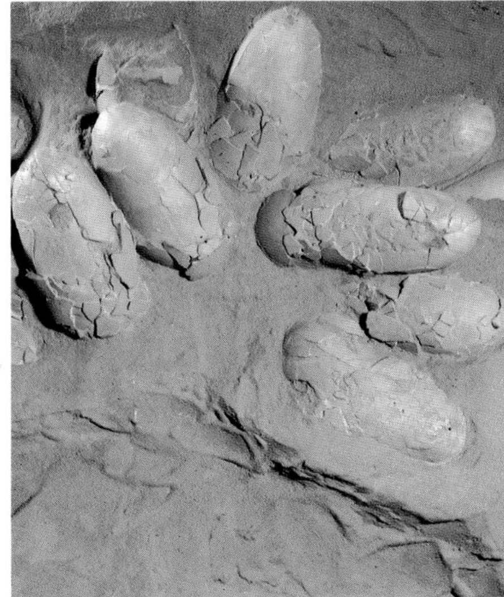

► *A nest of the fossil eggs of* Protoceratops. *The eggs are 8 inches long and were laid in a hollow scooped out of the sand. The female* Protoceratops *probably covered them with sand and let them hatch in the sun's heat.*

◄ *Workers in the early part of this century had to use a pulley and muscle power to raise the heavy fossil thigh bone of a* Diplodocus.

In 1677 Dr. Robert Plot was the first person to describe a dinosaur bone.

In 1822 Mary Mantell found some fossil teeth in a pile of stones by the roadside. They belonged to an *Iguanodon*.

Dr. Gideon Mantell described the plant-eater *Iguanodon*, the second dinosaur to get a scientific name.

Sir Richard Owen invented the name "dinosaur" in 1841. He later named ten kinds of dinosaur.

Othniel Marsh uncovered 25 new kinds of dinosaur in North America toward the end of the 19th century.

Edward Cope was Marsh's bitter rival in the the race to discover the most new kinds of dinosaurs.

to a group of mighty, prehistoric reptiles. In 1841, he named the group **dinosaurs**, which comes from two Greek words that mean "fearful reptiles."

Monsters from North America

More dinosaur bones were discovered in England and other European countries throughout the rest of the 1800s, but the most exciting finds began to come from North America.

In 1877, two school teachers independently found huge fossil bones in Colorado. One showed his finds to Othniel Marsh, a wealthy American **paleontologist**. The other showed what he had found to Marsh's rival, Edward Cope. Marsh and Cope began a race to see who could dig up the most, and the largest, dinosaur fossils. Armed against attacks by Indians, their teams of fossil hunters scoured the West. Marsh really won the race, discovering 25 "brand-new" kinds of dinosaur, compared to only 13 for Cope. Their discoveries laid the groundwork for what we know today about the Age of Dinosaurs.

In the 1880s, more dinosaur bones were found in the Canadian province of Alberta, and since 1900, fossil hunts have uncovered dinosaur fossils on every continent of the globe.

Hunting dinosaurs today

Today's fossil hunters may have tools the fossil hunters of the 1800s would have envied, but people still discover fossils in much the same way.

First, they must find rocks that were formed in the time of dinosaurs, some 65 to 230 million years ago. The best hunting grounds are deserts, cliffs, and quarries where no soil hides the rocks beneath. Since 1950 dozens of new dinosaurs have come

▼ *This immense* Brachiosaurus *skeleton towers over visitors to the Humboldt Museum in Berlin. The skeleton almost fills the room that was built for it. It is the world's largest mounted dinosaur skeleton.*

◀ *(facing page) Early efforts to reconstruct prehistoric animals were often inaccurate.* Iguanodon *(center) is shown here with a horn on its nose!*

IMPORTANT FINDS

DINOSAUR	WHEN NAMED
Megalosaurus	1824
Iguanodon	1825
Hadrosaurus	1858
Hypsilophodon	1869
Allosaurus	1877
Apatosaurus	1877
Stegosaurus	1877
Diplodocus	1878
Triceratops	1889
Brachiosaurus	1903
Tyrannosaurus	1905
Ankylosaurus	1908
Protoceratops	1923
Pachycephalosaurus	1943
Deinonychus	1969
Baryonyx	1986

from the dry regions in Argentina, Canada, China, Mongolia, Australia, and the United States.

Experienced fossil hunters walk slowly, staring at the ground. The clues they are looking for are ancient teeth or bits of bone lying just on the surface. Such a fossil may be no bigger than your thumb and could easily be mistaken for a shiny or spongy-looking stone. The fossils were once embedded in a layer of rock until frost or rain began to break it up. When freed, many fossils are washed downhill and this makes the floors of gullies excellent hunting grounds.

When experts find a fossil, they know more may lie higher up the slope. Patiently, they must search the rocks above. If they are lucky, they will find most of a dinosaur skeleton still embedded in a layer of rock. But finding it is often the easy part. Freeing the bones may be much more difficult.

Collecting fossils

Digging up a fossil dinosaur is hard work. The bones may be difficult to get to. Rocks can often be as hard as a brick and the bones so soft that they crumble between your fingers. Scientists have to solve the problem of how to free these ancient bones without damaging them.

▼ *A Polish scientist carefully chips away soft rock from the backbone of a big flesh-eating dinosaur that once lived in what is now the Gobi Desert.*

If the ground is fairly soft, the fossil hunters begin by digging around the bones. This helps them judge the shape and size of the skeleton. Often much of it is missing. If the dinosaur is small and is lying in soft ground, one or two people may be able to dig it out quite quickly. But a big dinosaur can take a large team weeks of work before it is freed.

First, the workers may have to bulldoze, or even blow up, several rock layers to get at the deeply buried bones. Then they use drills or picks and shovels to home in on the fossils. When they reach the bones, they use sharp awls or builder's trowels to chisel away any small, remaining bits of rock.

As they find the bones, the hunters photograph and number each one. They also make a chart to show where each bone lies. All this will help the laboratory workers who will piece the skeleton together later on.

Removing the bones is another tricky job. A large skeleton is sometimes cut out of the rock in blocks of stone with the bones still inside. Big bones are cushioned with plastic foam or sackcloth soaked in plaster, while small, fragile fossils get a coat of glue or resin to make them strong. The bones need to be well protected; their next move could be a long and bumpy ride before they reach a safe home in a museum.

▲ *A bonehead's skull lies embedded in rock before being removed and sent to a museum for careful study. Fossil remains such as this help scientists work out what the dinosaurs looked like and how they lived.*

▲ *Digging up dinosaurs can mean spending weeks in hot, dry countryside far from any town.*

▲ *Scientists take photographs of the uncovered bones to show exactly how they were buried.*

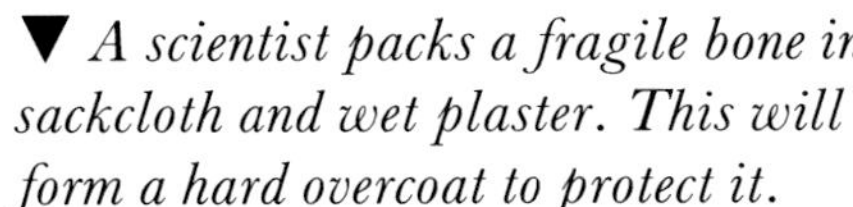

▼ *A scientist packs a fragile bone in sackcloth and wet plaster. This will form a hard overcoat to protect it.*

▼ *Workers load the heavy plaster-covered bones onto a truck ready to be transported to the museum.*

FINDING FOSSILS

Anyone can be a fossil hunter. The best hunting grounds are slopes where layered rocks such as shales and limestones show up on the surface. (Remember to keep away from high cliffs where you might fall or where rocks might fall on you.) To collect fossils you will need: a hammer and chisel, a builder's trowel, an old paintbrush and toothbrush, a notebook and pencil, and an old newspaper. Use your hammer to break open pieces of stone, and your trowel and paintbrush to clean away any loose dirt. If you find a fossil, write down in your notebook where and when you found it and wrap it up in some newspaper. At home, use an old toothbrush to clean your finds. You should then write a label for the fossil, saying what it is, where you found it, and how old it is. Your local museum or library will be able to help you find this information. Finally, you can store your fossil finds in cardboard trays made from small boxes or in a special drawer.

In the museum

It can take years of work in a museum laboratory before experts learn what a dinosaur looked like and how it lived.

First, laboratory technicians called preparators remove the protective wrappings from the bones. Power tools and chemicals then help them to get rid of any unwanted rock. Pneumatic chisels chip rock away. Jets of gas fire powder that sand-blasts stone. Acid dissolves some rock but leaves fossil bones unharmed.

Once the bones have been cleaned, paleontologists try to work out what kind of animal they came from. To do this they compare the new bones with bones from other dinosaurs. This will tell them if they belong to a previously undiscovered dinosaur or to one that has already been named. Scientists usually give a new dinosaur a scientific name using Greek or Latin words that describe something special about it. For example, *Baryonyx* ("heavy claw") was named after its huge claw.

With luck, the preparators will recover enough of a dinosaur skeleton to make rebuilding it worthwhile. Anatomists work

▼ *All that remains of the plant-eater* Stegosaurus *may be a jumbled mass of fossil bones and bony plates embedded in a slab of rock. To discover what the creature once looked like, scientists must first find out how these bones and plates were arranged. This difficult task is rather like putting together a model when many of the pieces are missing.*

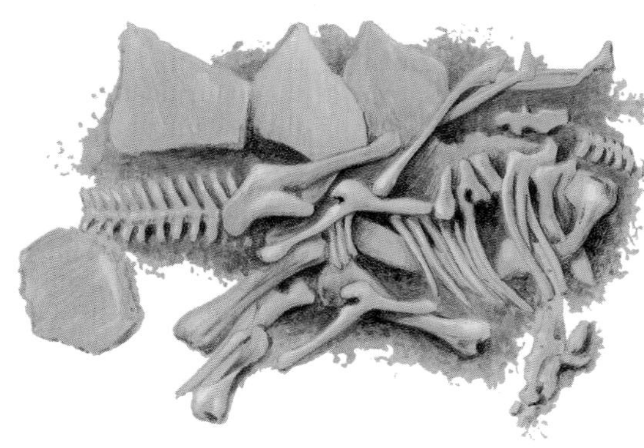

► *The shape of the bones helps scientists work out how they once fitted together (although sometimes a little intelligent guesswork is also needed)! Short, spiky bones formed the backbone and curved, narrow ribs guarded* Stegosaurus's *internal organs. Strong hip and shoulder bones would have supported the dinosaur's solid limb bones.*

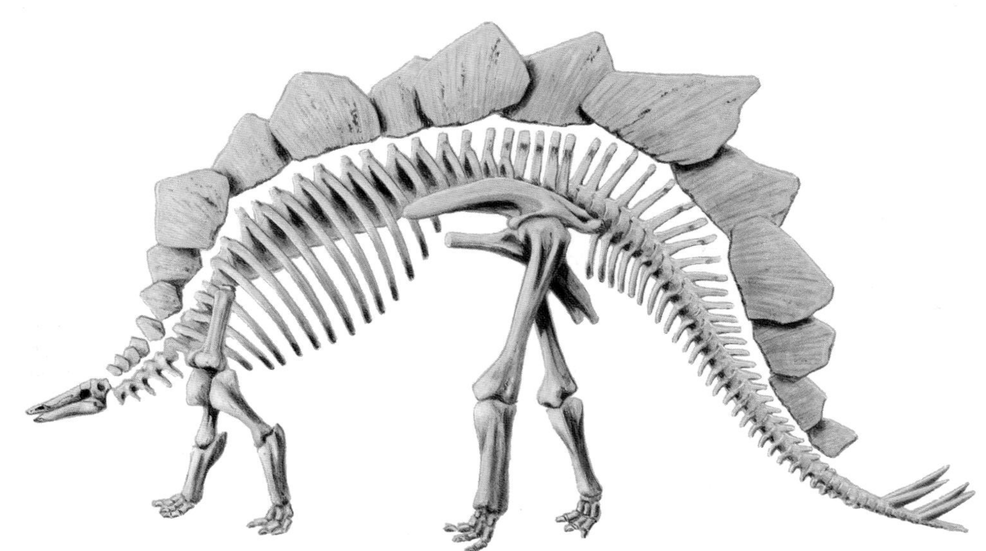

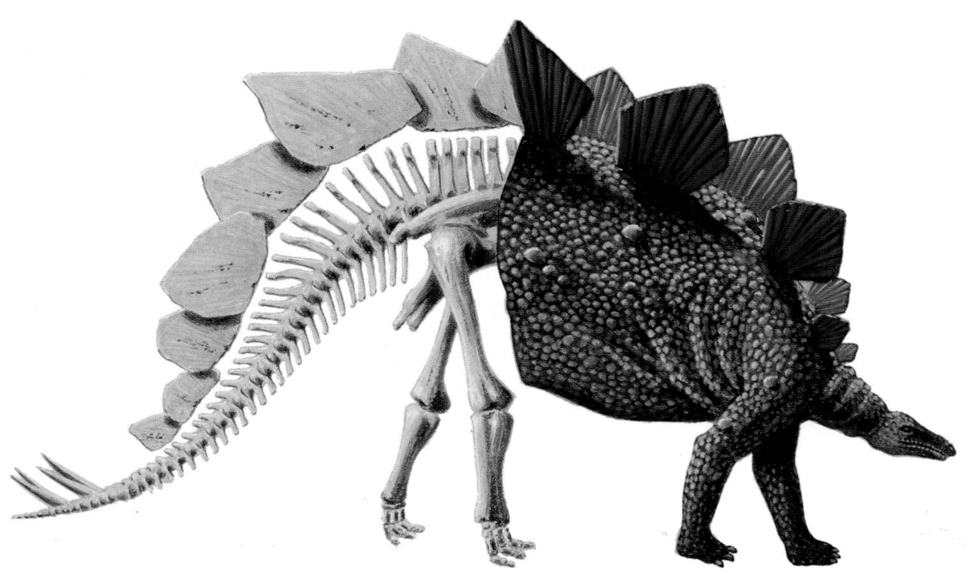

◄ *Once the skeleton has been rebuilt, experts can make a model of the whole dinosaur. Grooves on the bones show where muscles were attached. Often, comparing a dinosaur with a living animal can give scientists helpful clues. Very little evidence exists as to what dinosaur skin was like, but it probably had scales, and its color may have blended with the dinosaur's surroundings.*

out how the bones were arranged inside the living animal. Museum staff then fit the bits together, using glass-fiber models to replace any missing pieces. A scaffolding of metal rods and clamps is built to support the heavy bones. Erecting a big dinosaur skeleton may take months!

Understanding dinosaurs

Most of us only notice the sheer size of a big museum dinosaur. But its bones tell paleontologists a great deal more than just how big it was. The eye sockets, braincase, jaws, teeth, and other parts of the skull can tell us how well a dinosaur could see, hear, smell, and think, and whether it ate plants or other animals. Bumps and ridges on the limb bones reveal where big, strong muscles were attached. By carefully studying such telltale signs, scientists can work out the long-dead creature's shape and size and how it stood. Sculptors can then make a lifelike scale model of the animal.

Scientists have yet more clues to help them understand the dinosaurs. Damaged bones reveal that some individuals suffered from diseases and that others survived terrible wounds. Fossil skin imprints show that one kind of dinosaur had a pebbly-patterned hide, while another's skin was armed with horny plates and spikes. Fossil footprints can tell us how fast dinosaurs ran. Fossil eggs and babies hint at how they bred.

Piecing together all these clues has made it possible to tell the exciting story of the dinosaurs.

▲ *A worker at Dinosaur National Monument in Utah carefully uses a hammer and chisel to bring the shoulder blade of a* Camarasaurus *into relief.*

▼ *Very often casts are made of dinosaur bones. First a rubber mold is made. This is then filled with plaster. Once the cast has set, it can be used to make new models of the dinosaur, perhaps in different poses.*

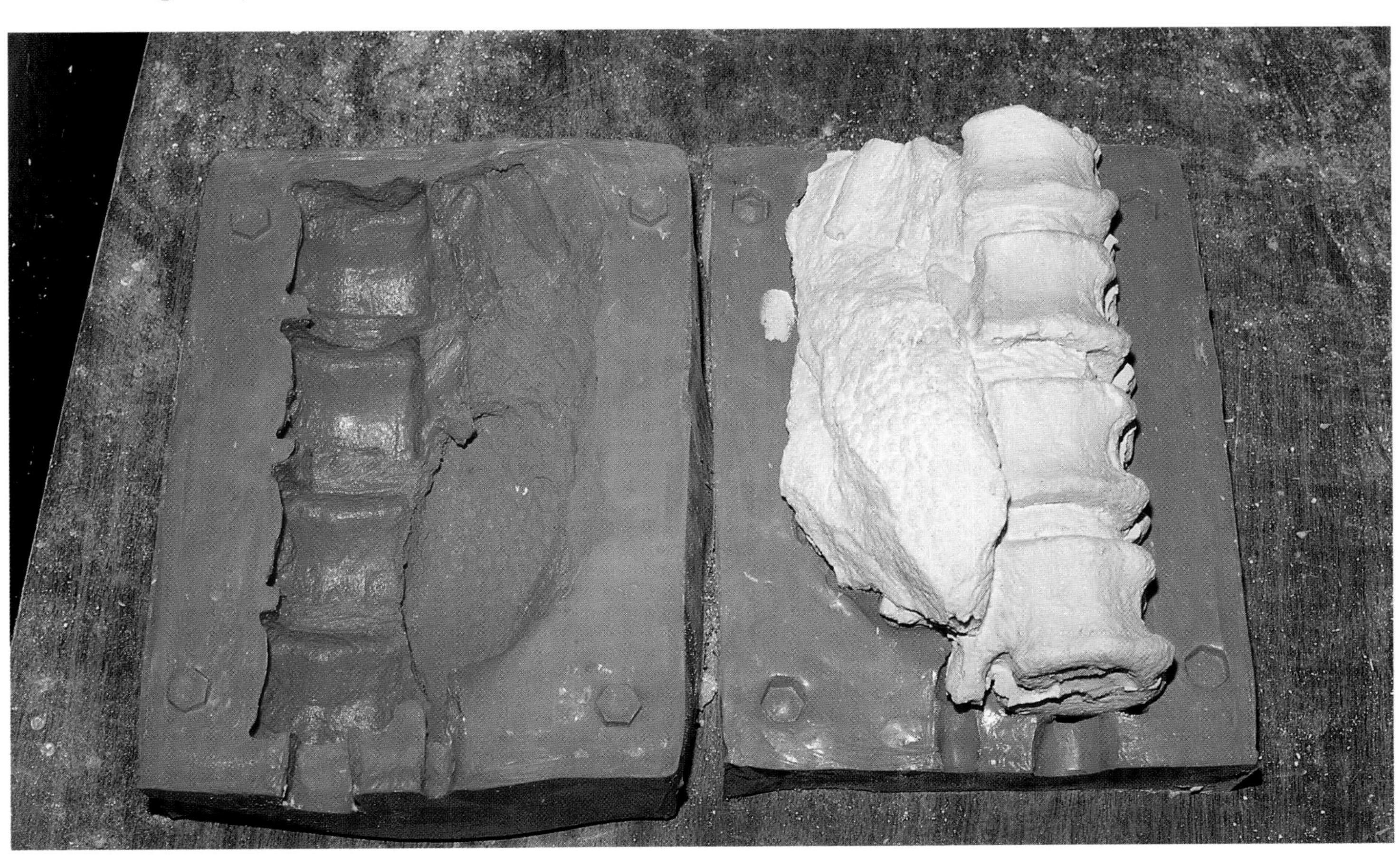

life begins

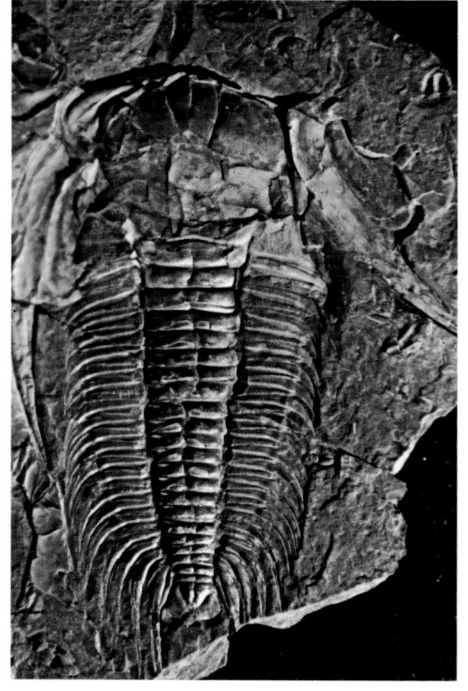

▲ *This fossil trilobite is about 550 million years old. Trilobites resembled woodlice, but they lived under the sea.*

The first true dinosaurs appeared about 230 million years ago. But to find out how and why we must go even further back in time. We learn that from tiny forms of life came fishes, then **amphibians**, then **reptiles**, one group of which eventually gave rise to the dinosaurs.

The clues to this fascinating story lie in sedimentary rocks formed from layers of mud and silt that settled on the floors of lakes and seas millions of years ago. Some cliffs are like a layer cake of sedimentary rock. The top layer is usually the youngest and the lowest layer the oldest.

Each layer may hold the fossilized remains of plants and animals that were alive when that layer was formed. By studying the different layers, **geologists** found that, over millions of years, tiny, simple **organisms** had given rise to bigger, more complicated living things such as plants and animals. As time passed, early **species** of plants and animals died out to be replaced by new ones that were better adapted to survive in the changing conditions of their world.

The earth's ages

Geologists divide the history of the earth into **eras**. Dinosaurs lived in the **Mesozoic era**, or "Age of Middle Life," sometimes called the Age of Dinosaurs. The Mesozoic era lasted from 248 to 65 million years ago. But the story of the dinosaurs,

▼ *A "tree of life" shows the evolution of plants and animals. The major groups are indicated by different colored bands. Plants, fungi, and single-celled bacteria are shown in green, the animals without a backbone in blue, and the animals with a backbone in red.*

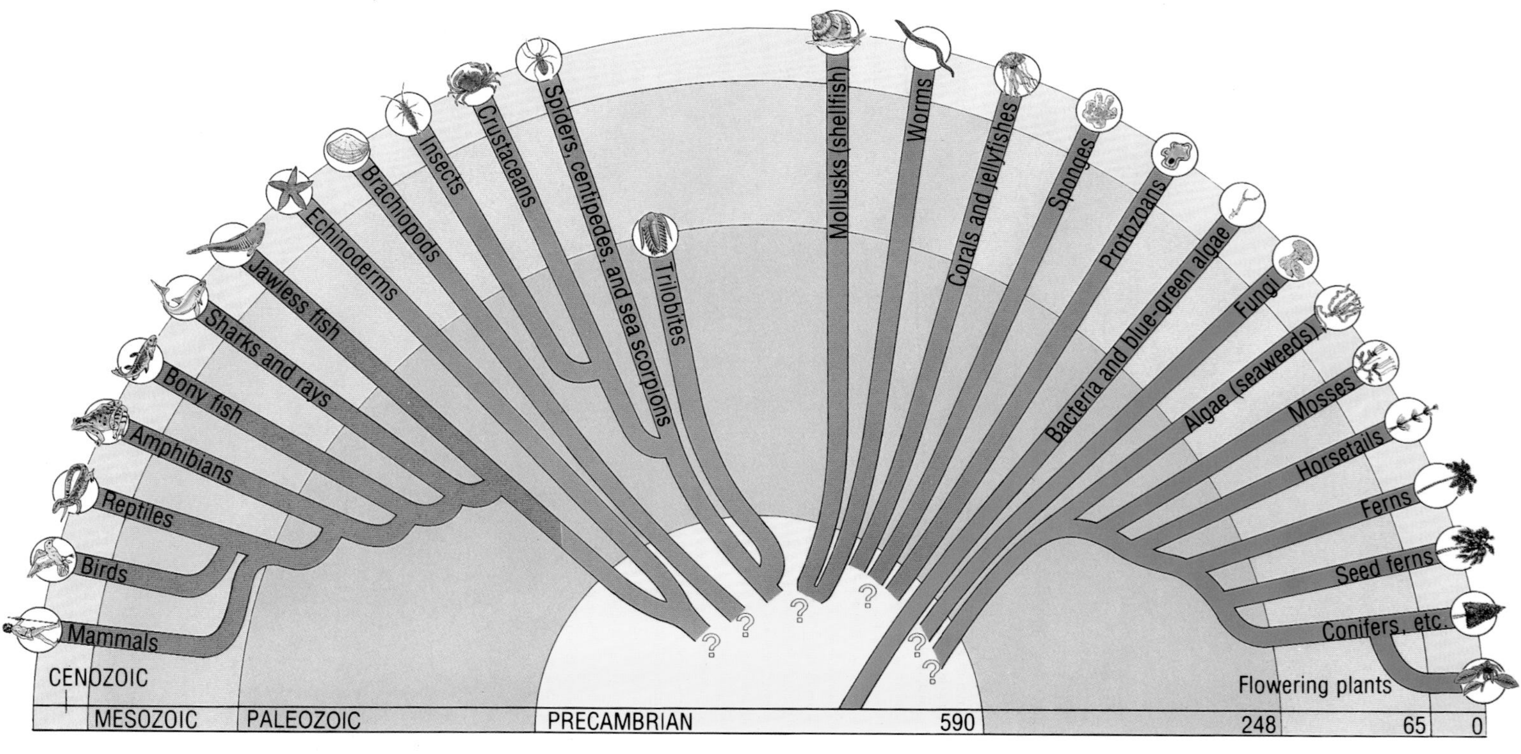

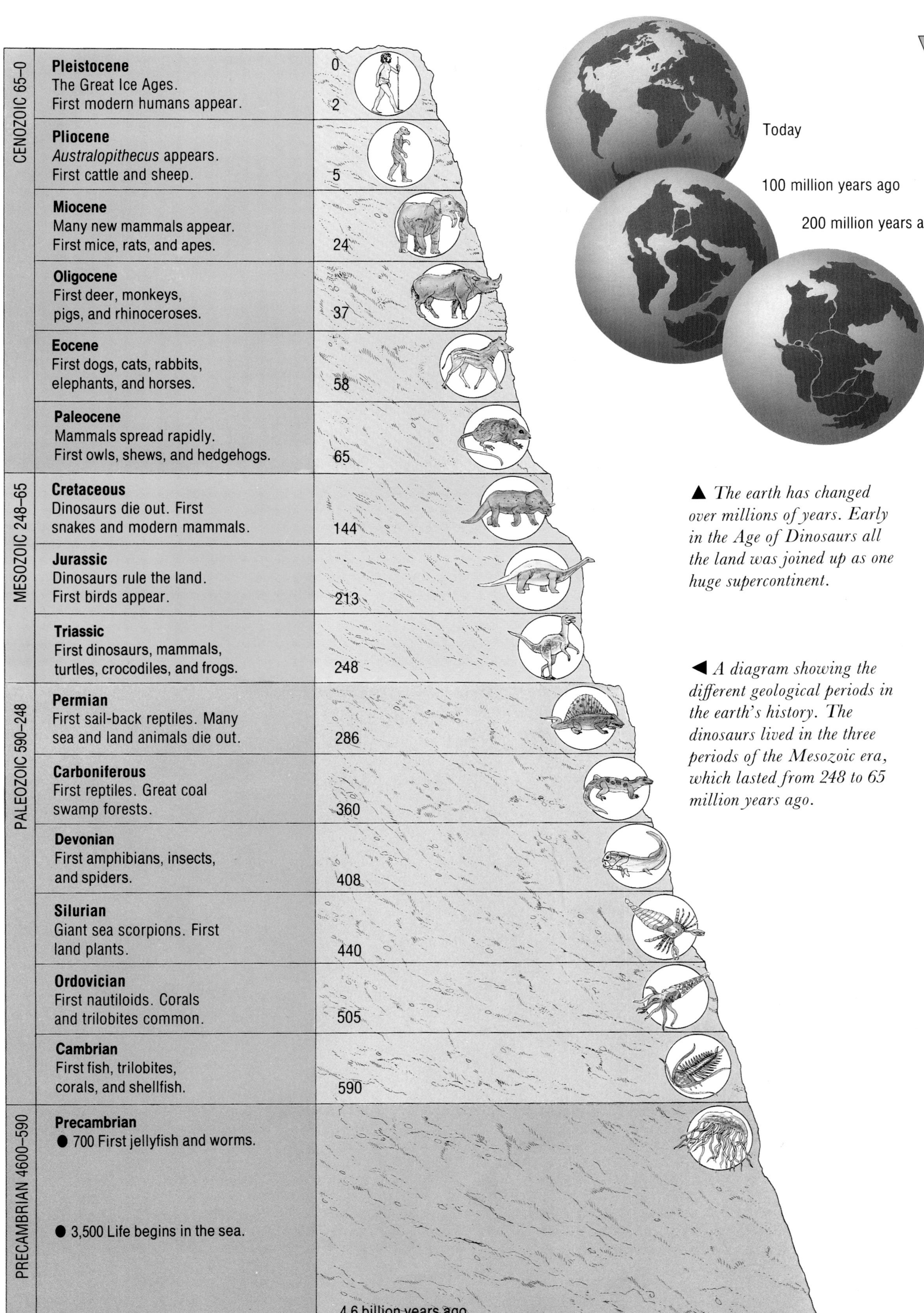

▲ *The earth has changed over millions of years. Early in the Age of Dinosaurs all the land was joined up as one huge supercontinent.*

◀ *A diagram showing the different geological periods in the earth's history. The dinosaurs lived in the three periods of the Mesozoic era, which lasted from 248 to 65 million years ago.*

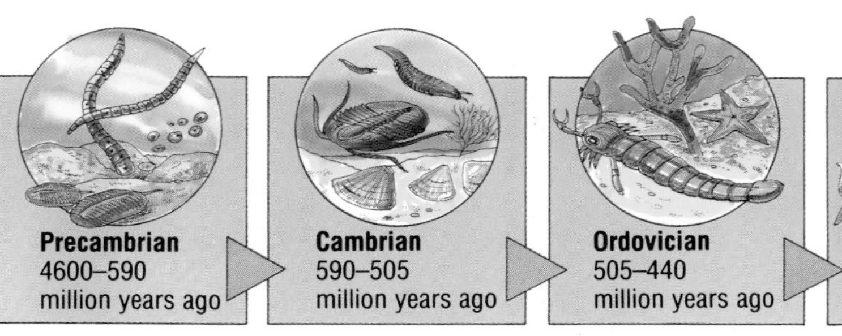

◀ *The history of life under the sea. From one-celled animals came trilobites and brachiopods in the Cambrian period. Sea scorpions and corals followed in the Ordovician and Silurian periods.*

like that of all living things, really started in the mysterious eras of **Precambrian** time – the earth's first 4 billion years.

About 4.6 billion years ago a whirling mass of dust and rock came together to create our planet. Immense heat melted its rocky ingredients until the earth was just a molten ball. Above it hung a steamy atmosphere of suffocating gases. In time the surface cooled and hardened into rock and the steam cooled into droplets that fell as rain. This downpour lasted centuries and filled great hollows in the ground with oceans.

Specks of life

Life probably started in the sea. Sunlight and lightning supplied energy to build living things from chemicals in the prehistoric oceans. First, heat energy joined together certain kinds of **atoms** – the tiny, invisible building blocks of which everything is made – to form **molecules** of simple substances. Some formed sugars and **amino acids** that joined up to build **proteins** – substances found in all living things. Later came **nucleic acids**. These then multiplied by splitting in two and copying themselves. This is how the earliest living things reproduced. Later, came more complicated organisms made up of strings of nucleic acid molecules in a protein-and-water coat. These are called **cells**.

These little organisms fed on the ready-made proteins in the sea. There was a danger that all the proteins would be used up and that all the living things would starve to death. But at some point, one of the early organisms gave rise to the tiny, plantlike **blue-green algae**. These used the energy in sunlight to make their own food from common chemicals in the sea. True plants, which evolved later, also make their food in this way. This process is called **photosynthesis**. Blue-green algae and plants both gave off oxygen as waste. This made the air fit to breathe for the first animals – living things that get food by eating plants or one another.

Animals of ancient seas

Animals may have evolved from one-celled organisms that had "gone wrong." When these organisms split to multiply, their cells stayed stuck together, creating larger organisms that were made up of many cells. Some organisms developed different kinds of cell, each made for feeding, moving, or some other special task.

▼ *These fossil shells belonged to brachiopods, the most common shellfish in Cambrian times.*

▼ *A scene from a Silurian coral reef. Among the horn coral and sea lilies, trilobites scavenged for food in the mud. The fierce hunter* Pterygotus *was a sea scorpion that grew up to 6 feet long.*

Horn coral

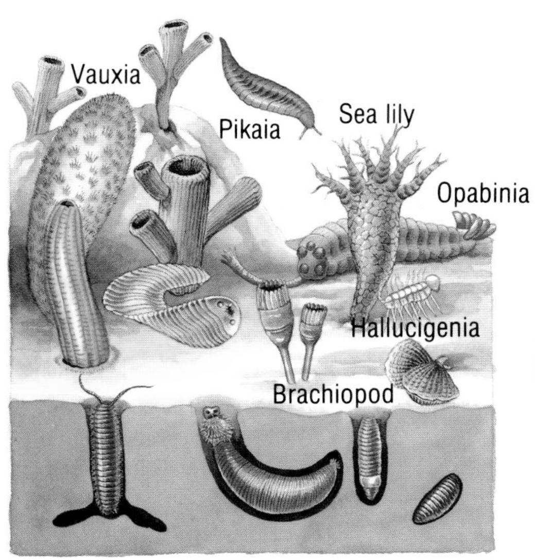

▲ *Sponges such as* Vauxia, *worms and the many-legged* Opabinia *and* Hallucigenia *lived on the Cambrian sea bed.*

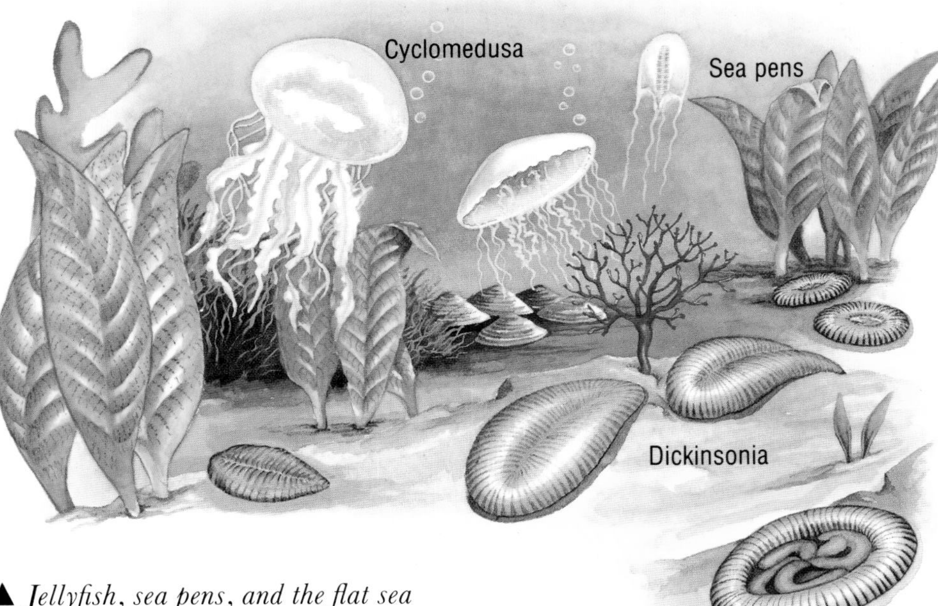

▲ *Jellyfish, sea pens, and the flat sea worm* Dickinsonia *lived 680 million years ago in a sea that covered what is now South Austrialia.*

▼ *Trilobite fossils have been found in rocks that date from the Cambrian through to the Permian periods. Trilobites grew between half an inch and 15 inches long.*

These early animals lived about a billion years ago. But it was only in the **Paleozoic era**, or "Age of Ancient Life" (590 to 248 million years ago), that creatures grew plentiful. Scientists divide this era into six **periods**: **Cambrian**, **Ordovician**, **Silurian**, **Devonian**, **Carboniferous**, and **Permian**. For the first two, animals lived only under water.

By Cambrian times (590 to 505 million years ago), most of the main groups of **invertebrates** – animals with no backbone – had appeared. The Cambrian seas teemed with soft-bodied jellyfish and worms. **Trilobites** and **brachiopods**,

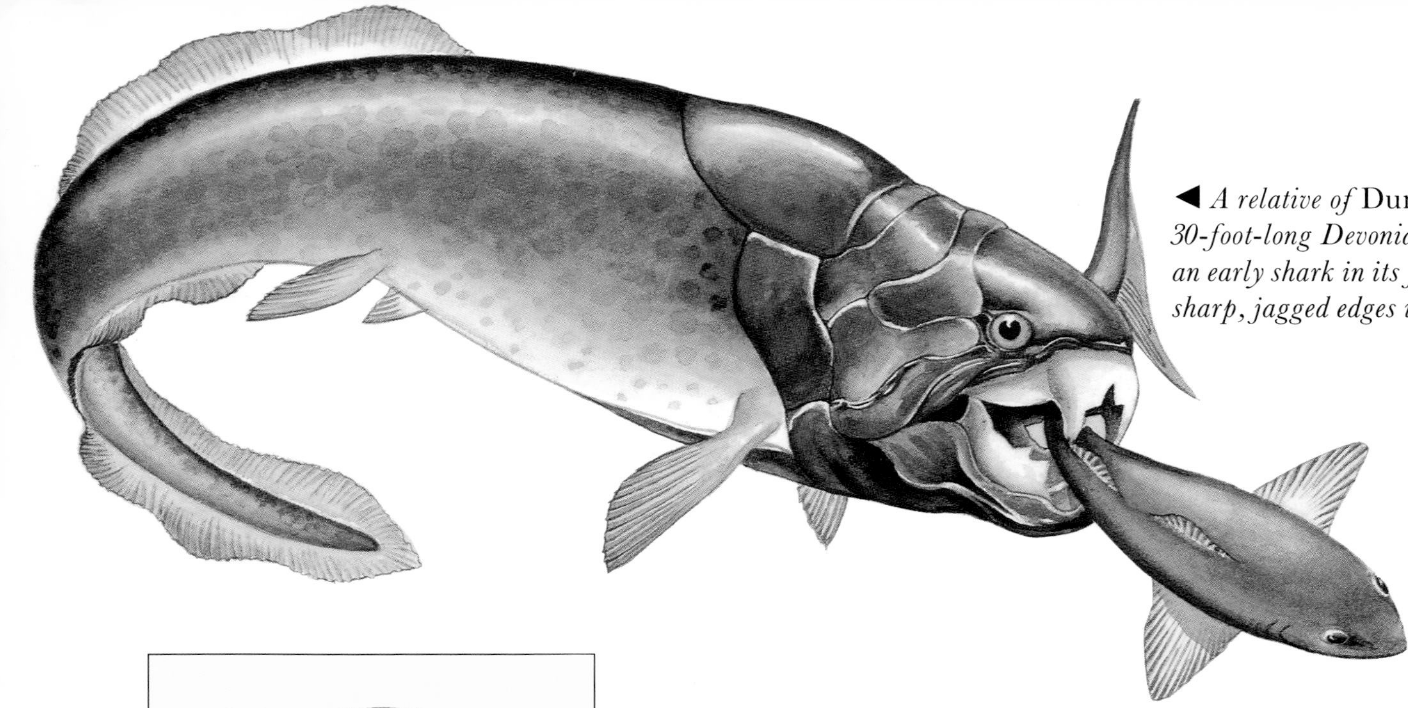

◀ *A relative of* Dunkleosteus, *a 30-foot-long Devonian fish, seizes an early shark in its jaws. These had sharp, jagged edges instead of teeth.*

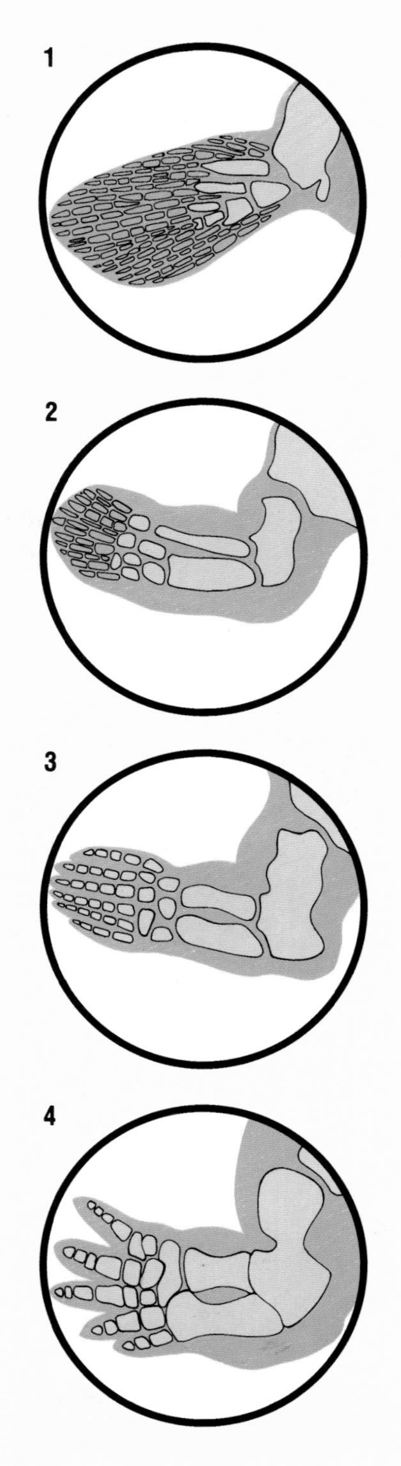

protected by hard shells, lived on the seabed. During the Ordovician period (505 to 440 million years ago), **mollusks**, corals, and early relatives of the squid and octopus developed. An ancestor of the starfish had also given rise to small **vertebrates** – creatures with a bony skeleton.

An inside skeleton has huge advantages over a hard shell. Like a crab's shell, a fish's skeleton supports its body and guards its vital organs. But a fish can move around more freely than a crab or mollusk. Also, a growing crab must shed its shell from time to time, so losing its protection and support. Fish never face that problem.

One day, strong, internal skeletons would prop up the dinosaurs, the heaviest animals that ever stood on land.

◀ *The four drawings show how the bones of a fish's fin (1) evolved (2 and 3) into an amphibian's leg bones (4). The basic limb structure remains the same, but the bone sizes alter.*

▼ *The mudskipper can gulp air and chase prey across the mud at low tide. These small fish help scientists to explain how life may have moved from the water onto the land.*

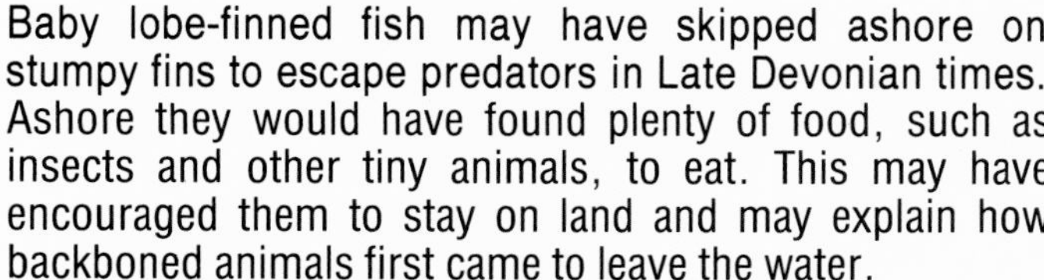

Baby lobe-finned fish may have skipped ashore on stumpy fins to escape predators in Late Devonian times. Ashore they would have found plenty of food, such as insects and other tiny animals, to eat. This may have encouraged them to stay on land and may explain how backboned animals first came to leave the water.

Early amphibians such as *Ichthyostega* probably evolved from lobe-finned fish. The early amphibians had scaly bodies, sprawling limbs, and long tails. Although they had lungs for breathing air, animals such as *Ichthyostega* may still have spent much of their time in the water and would have laid their eggs there.

Life invades the land

During Silurian times (440 to 408 million years ago), water plants and animals began to colonize the land. Seaweeds would have shriveled up on land, but some early water plants gave rise to land plants. These had stiff stems that could reach up to the light and roots to suck up nourishment and water. A waterproof "skin" kept these pioneers from drying out.

Where plants had led, animals could follow, because, in one way or another, all animals depend on plants for food. The first land animals were **arthropods** – invertebrates with jointed legs. Among them were the ancestors of those modern creepy-crawlies: scorpions, millipedes, and woodlice.

By Devonian times (408 to 360 million years ago), the first backboned animals had followed the arthropods onto the land. These vertebrates were fish that hauled themselves from shallow pools on strong, fleshy, lobe-shaped fins. The **lobe-finned fishes** had lungs, so they could breathe in open air as well as under water.

From fins to legs

It seems unlikely that lobe-fins lingered out of water for very long. They were fish, after all. One kind of lobe-fin, however, gave rise to the first amphibians. These were backboned animals with fishlike scales and legs that had evolved from fins. The early amphibians may have sprawled awkwardly across the ground, but they were the first vertebrates with limbs designed specially for use on land. Their skeletons already looked more like a dinosaur's bony framework, but still more changes would be needed to produce the dinosaurs.

▼ *The leaves of a prehistoric horsetail are clearly defined in this fossil. Plants from the Carboniferous period also survive as traces left in coal. Coal is made of the compressed remains of prehistoric vegetation.*

► *Diadectes and Seymouria were two Permian amphibians that seem to have been completely adapted for life on land. Diadectes's sturdy limbs and blunt, peglike teeth suggest that it moved quite quickly and that it fed on roots and plants, not insects.*

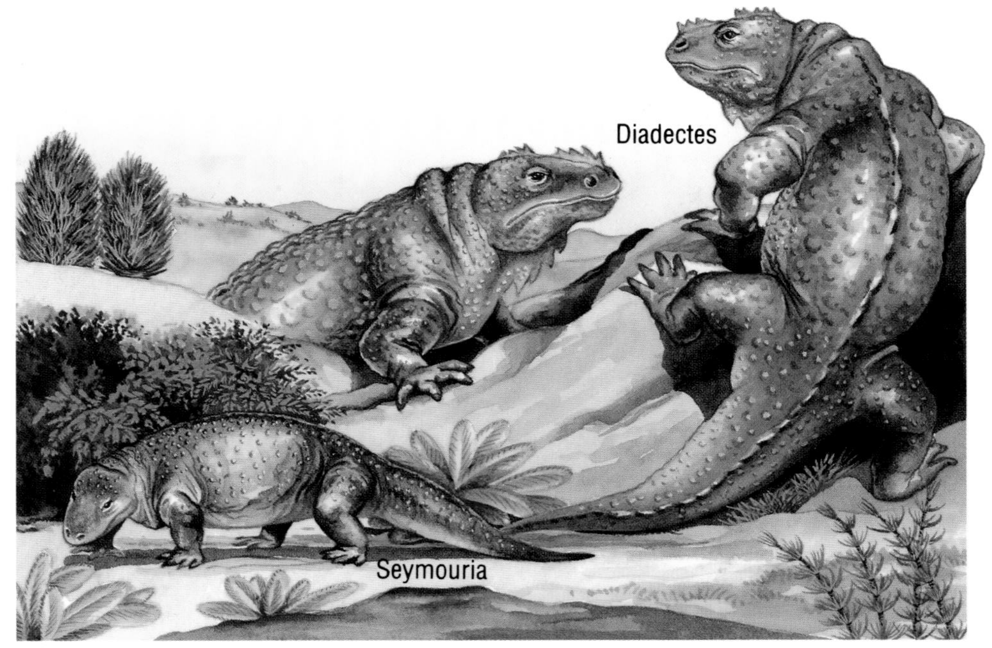

▼ *The small Carboniferous amphibian Branchiosaurus had feathery gills on the side of its neck. These show that it could breathe underwater. Scientists are unsure whether Branchiosaurus was a young tadpole or whether it was a grown animal that always lived underwater.*

Amphibians teemed in the warm forests of the Carboniferous period (360 to 286 million years ago). They wallowed in and out of swampy pools while above them soared huge horsetail plants, ferns higher than a house, and clubmosses that grew as tall as trees with trunks as thick as pillars. Giant millipedes that grew up to 6 feet long and other early insects hunted for food amongst the rotting leaves and plants on the forest floor. Dragonflies with the longest wings of any known insect zoomed overhead.

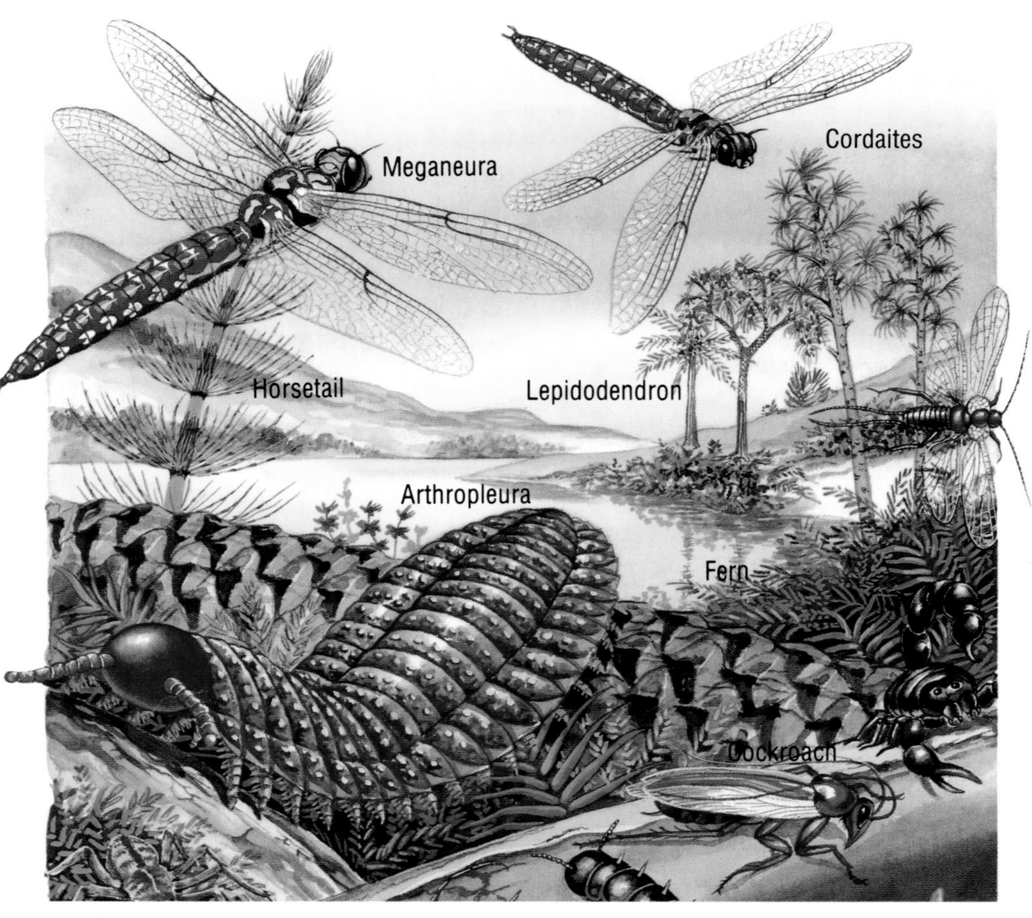

► *Plants and insects such as these shared the Carboniferous swamp forests with early amphibians and the first reptiles. Cordaites and the clubmoss Lepidodendron were trees that stood 100 feet tall. Among the fallen logs crawled early cockroaches, scorpions, centipedes, and the giant millipede Arthropleura. At 6 feet long, this was the largest of all arthropods. Above flew the immense dragonfly Meganeura. This swift hunter had a wingspan of 28 inches and ate flying stoneflies and other insects.*

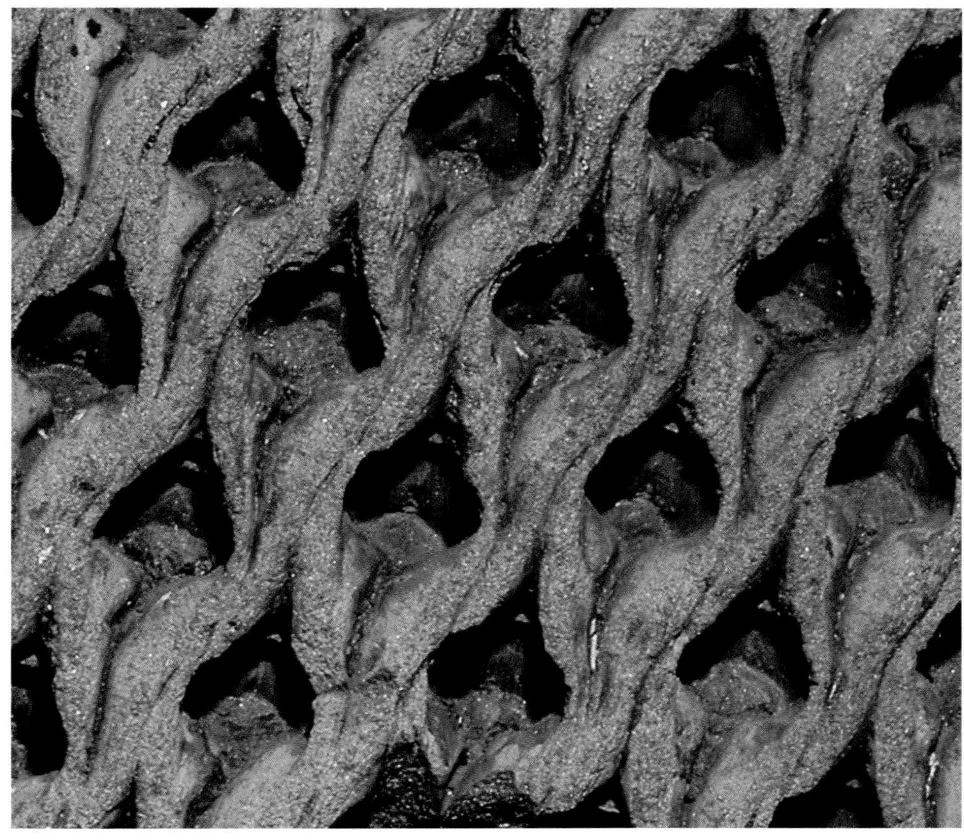

◀ *The patterned trunk of a giant clubmoss has been preserved in this fossil. Giant clubmosses had trunks that grew up to 6 feet in diameter. They grew in the swampy forests of Carboniferous times.*

Reptiles arrive

Amphibians shared their watery forests with small land animals that looked rather like lizards. These were the world's first reptiles. Reptiles evolved from advanced amphibians that were better equipped for life on land than their ancestors. These advanced amphibians had sturdy limb bones worked by powerful muscles. Eardrums helped them hear in air and tear glands moistened their eyes. But even these advanced amphibians had to lay their eggs in water to prevent them drying out. Reptiles were the first vertebrates to live *and breed* away from lakes or rivers.

Built for life on land

Reptiles are better adapted for life on land than amphibians. Their waterproof scales keep the inside of their bodies comfortably moist. Amphibians, on the other hand, have skins that dry out quickly in warm, dry air. Reptiles also have stronger hearts and lungs that allow them to walk and run better than amphibians.

But perhaps the most important difference between reptiles and amphibians is the ability to breed on land. A male reptile fertilizes an egg inside the female's body instead of shedding sperm haphazardly on eggs already laid in water. This is a far more efficient way of fertilizing an egg. A reptile's egg also has a leathery or hard shell with special linings that keep the baby reptile safely moist inside. An amphibian's egg has only a blob of jelly for protection and cannot survive out of water.

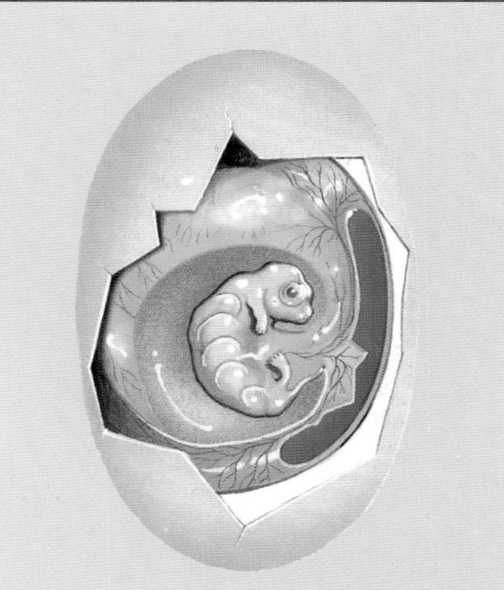

REPTILE EGGS

Reptile eggs (above) were far better adapted for life on land than amphibian eggs. Liquid inside the egg cushioned the embryo and stopped it from drying out, while the tough outer shell supported and protected it. The yolk acted as a food supply, nourishing the young reptile until it was ready to hatch. Baby reptiles emerge from their shells (below). The mother reptile probably laid her eggs in a hollow in the sand and let the heat of the sun hatch them. Modern reptiles, such as lizards, snakes, and turtles, still hatch their eggs in this way.

► *The two pelycosaurs* Dimetrodon *and* Edaphosaurus *lived in what is now Texas.* Dimetrodon *had sharp, meat-eating teeth and may have preyed on the plant-eating* Edaphosaurus. *Both animals had a tall sail of skin jutting up from their back. Scientists believe that they may have used this to control their body temperature.*

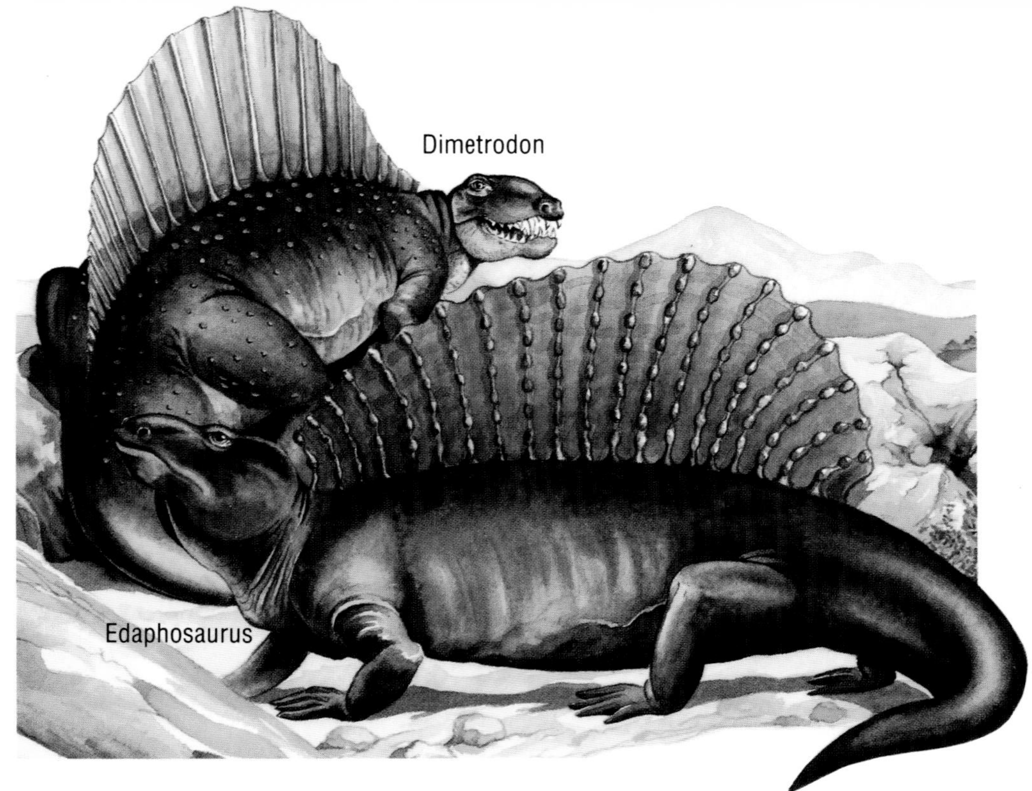

▲ *The tall, bony sail of a pelycosaur was covered in skin that was rich in blood vessels. When the reptile was cold, it would have turned sideways to the sun so that the blood vessels could take in heat. When it got too hot, the animal would have turned its back on the sun and the sail would have given off heat.*

Reptiles multiply

Deserts replaced swamps in Permian times (286 to 248 million years ago). As their watery homes dried up, amphibians grew scarcer. Reptiles, however, multiplied. Small, sharp-toothed creatures that hunted insects gave rise to larger, fiercer reptiles. These preyed on other big plant-eating reptiles.

As the reptiles diversified, one group came to be dominant. These were the **mammal-like reptiles**. One early group of

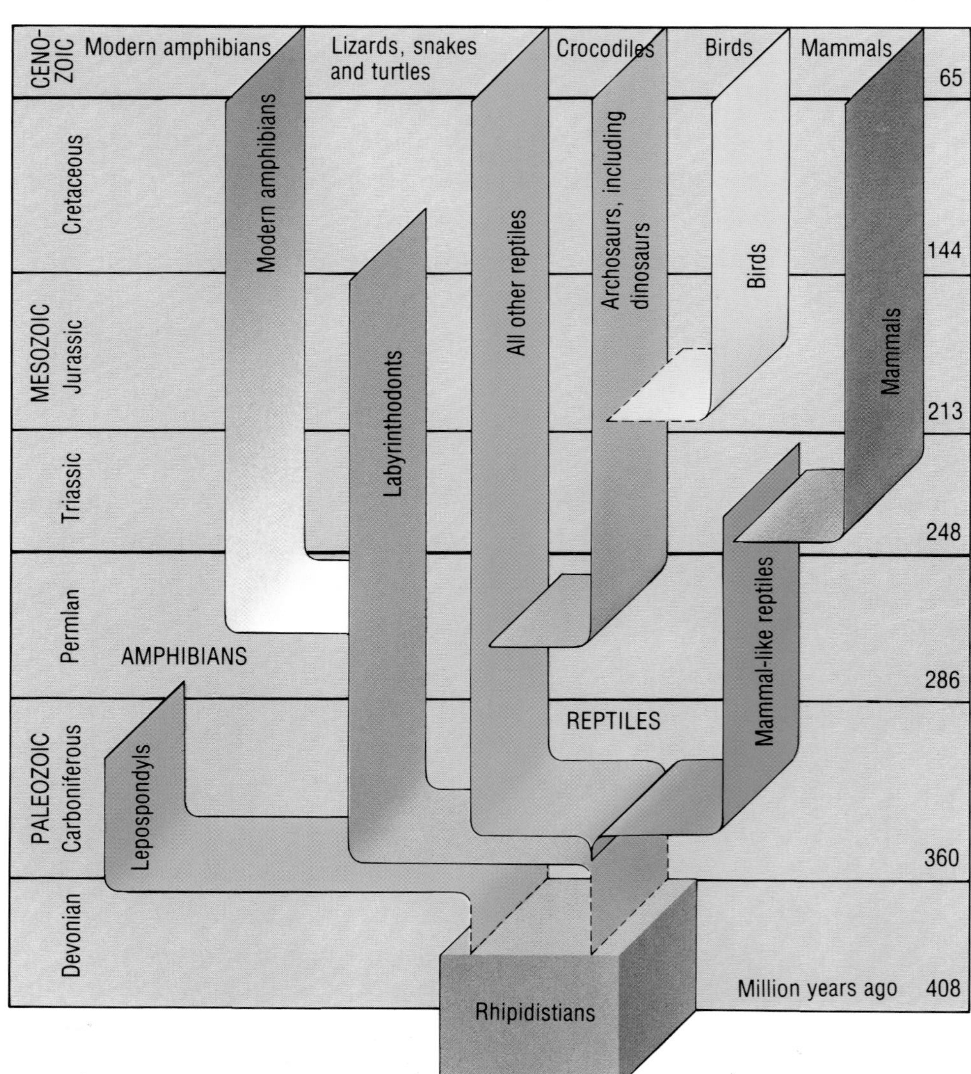

► *A simplified family tree shows how the dinosaurs were related to other groups of animals. The rhipidistians were the lobe-finned fishes that gave rise to two big groups of amphibians: the lepospondyls and the labyrinthodonts. Archosaur reptiles, including the dinosaurs, evolved from a group of reptiles that also gave rise to modern lizards and snakes. Modern mammals are descended from the mammal-like reptiles.*

mammal-like reptiles were the **pelycosaurs** ("basin reptiles"). Dozens of kinds of these creatures roamed what it now the southwest United States. Some of them, such as *Edaphosaurus* ("ground reptile"), were plant-eaters; others, such as *Dimetrodon* ("two-measure tooth"), fed on other reptiles. Most pelycosaurs had tall, bony spikes rising from their backbone. These supported a skin web, or sail. Scientists believe that they used this sail to control their body temperature.

▲ *The fierce therapsid reptile* Lycaenops *sinks its fangs into a plant-eating relative, the dicynodont* Dicynodon. *Such struggles took place in Late Permian southern Africa.*

The mammals' ancestors

From pelycosaurs came reptiles built much more like **mammals**. Skull holes like those found in mammals earned these the name **therapsids** ("mammal openings"). Among the later therapsids were reptiles that walked with their knees and elbows held below their body like a dog. These creatures almost certainly grew a hairy coat to keep their bodies warm and were probably **warm-blooded** in the way mammals are.

There were thousands of different kinds of therapsids. They were masters of the land for 40 million years and eventually gave rise to the mammals after the Paleozoic era ended. Then the terapsids mysteriously died out. Meanwhile, however, a new group of reptiles had developed. From them would come the new rulers of the land – the dinosaurs.

▼ *Two doglike* Cynognathus *crunch on the bones of a dead* Lystrosaurus. Lystrosaurus *resembled a hippopotamus and probably fed on plants growing in swamps. Both these kinds of therapsids lived early in the Triassic period, before the dinosaurs evolved.*

the age of dinosaurs

▲ *Crocodiles evolved from reptiles known as archosaurs. Unlike their sprawling ancestors, however, crocodiles can lift their bodies off the ground to run. This allows them to move quite quickly. When the dinosaurs evolved, they too were designed to move quickly on land.*

▼ *A warm-blooded lion must eat ten times as many antelope as a cold-blooded crocodile. Some scientists argue that dinosaurs were also warm-blooded because the numbers of flesh-eating and plant-eating dinosaurs seem similar to the figures for warm-blooded animals.*

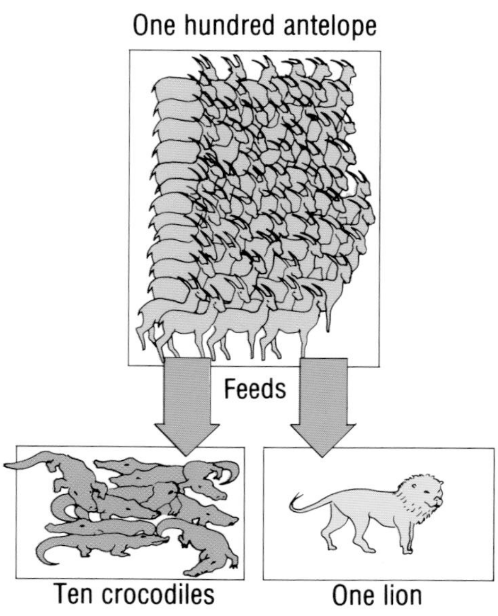

The first dinosaurs appeared early in the Mesozoic era, or Age of Dinosaurs (248 to 65 million years ago). At the start of the Mesozoic, the reptile line that led to the dinosaurs was already well established. From small, lizardlike animals the line split in two. One branch gave rise to lizards and snakes, the other to the **archosaurs**, or "ruling reptiles." Mesozoic archosaurs became masters of land, air, lakes, and rivers. Early kinds included the **thecodonts**, or "socket toothed" reptiles. From these came the crocodilians, dinosaurs, and **pterosaurs** ("winged reptiles"). Only crocodilians survive today.

Early ancestors

Among the best known early thecodonts was the sprawling, crocodilelike *Proterosuchus* ("first crocodile"). Later, came small, agile thecodonts with long hind limbs and knees and elbows that were fairly well tucked in to hold their bodies off the ground. This semi-erect posture allowed them to run more quickly than the early, sprawling thecodonts.

One of these later thecodonts was *Euparkeria* ("true Parker's"). *Euparkeria* resembled a light, agile, long-legged crocodile no bigger than a cat. It could rise on its hind limbs and run quite fast, balanced by its long, strong tail. *Ornithosuchus* ("bird crocodile") and little *Lagosuchus* ("rabbit crocodile") were thecodonts that walked and ran with their limbs tucked in even more beneath their bodies. Such creatures were the ancestors of the pterosaurs and dinosaurs.

Dinosaur posture

Dinosaurs had the same erect posture that *Lagosuchus* had. That means their limbs were well tucked in underneath their

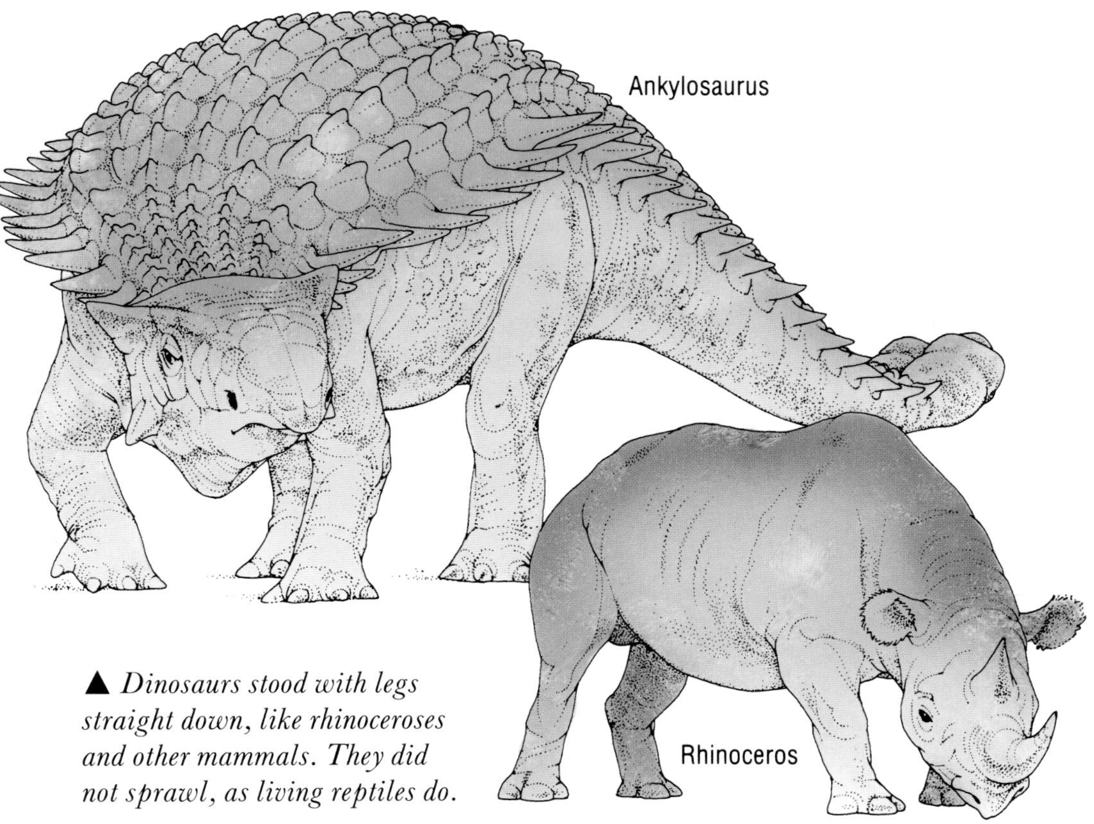

▲ *Dinosaurs stood with legs straight down, like rhinoceroses and other mammals. They did not sprawl, as living reptiles do.*

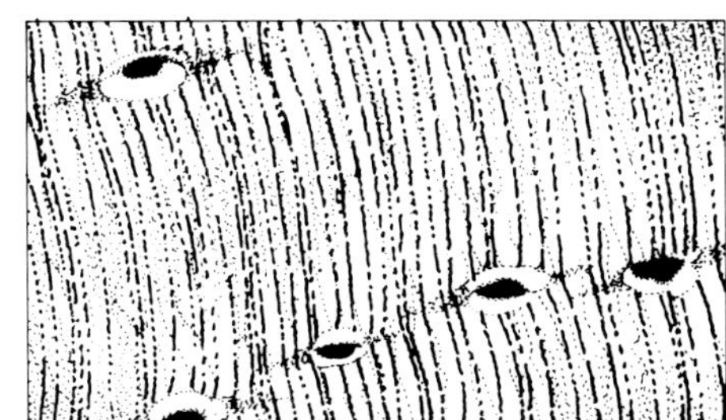

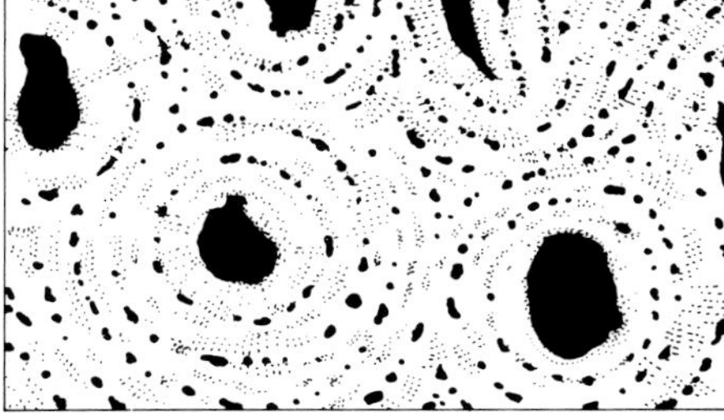

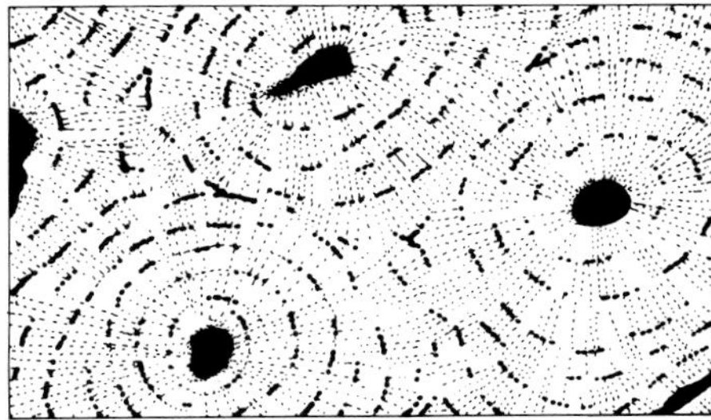

▲ *Cow and dinosaur bone contains rings but the lizard bone shows none. Some people think this means dinosaurs were warm-blooded.*

bodies, like a horse's. Scientists can tell this by studying their skeletons, especially the hip, thigh, leg, and foot bones. Each thigh bone turned in sharply at the top. This ball-shaped end fitted into a deep hole in the hip bone to form a ball-and-socket joint. Toes were long, ankles high, and the ankle joint was a straight hinge. The structure of their legs was one of the reasons for the dinosaurs' success. Unlike the sprawling thecodonts, they could take long strides and run much faster. Dinosaurs walked on their toes, like birds. Sprinting on their toes, early dinosaurs probably outran most other creatures. This meant they were quick at catching prey and escaping danger, which helped them to spread and multiply.

The great dinosaur puzzle

Scientists still puzzle over what the dinosaurs were really like. Their limb bones hint that many dinosaurs could run far and fast, like warm-blooded ostriches and horses. Ordinary reptiles can only run in short bursts because they are **cold-blooded**. Does this mean that the dinosaurs were warm-blooded? If so, dinosaurs were like no ordinary reptiles. Perhaps *small* dinosaurs were warm-blooded. But maybe bigger dinosaurs stayed warm and active because their bodies were able to store up so much heat from the sun that they never cooled down at night. We do not yet know the full answer.

Dinosaur groups

One thing we do know is that the dinosaurs can be divided into two main groups: the **saurischians** ("lizard-hips") and the **ornithischians** ("bird-hips"). The two groups are identified by their hip bones, as the names suggest. Saurischian

▼ *Dinosaurs form two main groups: saurischians and ornithischians. A saurischian's hip bones point in different directions. In ornithischians, the forward-pointing bone has swung around and points backward as well as forward.*

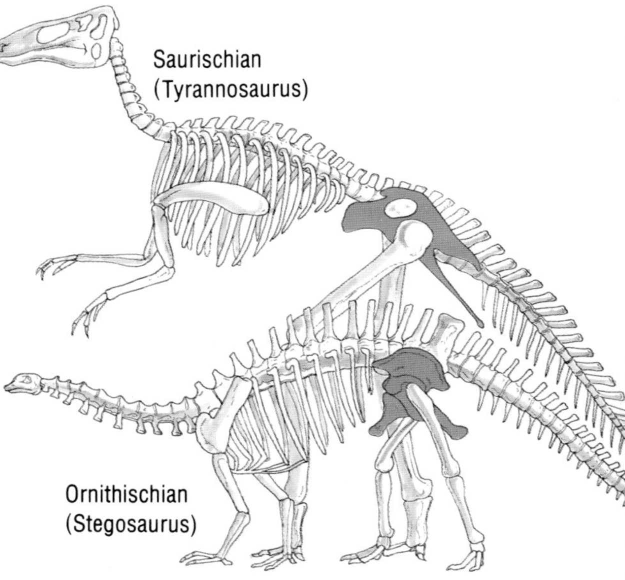

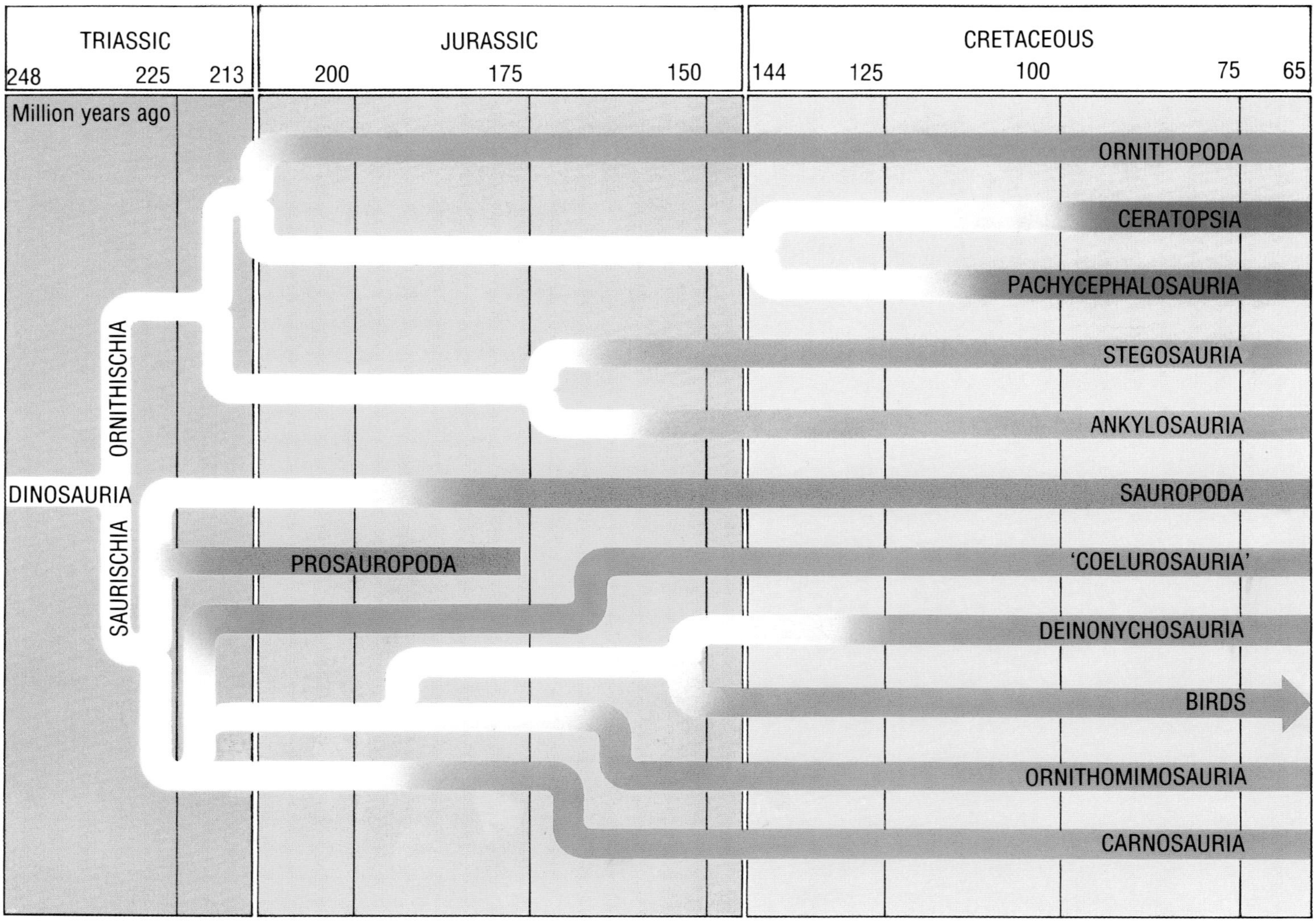

TRIASSIC
248 225 213
JURASSIC
200 175 150
CRETACEOUS
144 125 100 75 65
Million years ago
DINOSAURIA
ORNITHISCHIA
SAURISCHIA
ORNITHOPODA
CERATOPSIA
PACHYCEPHALOSAURIA
STEGOSAURIA
ANKYLOSAURIA
SAUROPODA
PROSAUROPODA
'COELUROSAURIA'
DEINONYCHOSAURIA
BIRDS
ORNITHOMIMOSAURIA
CARNOSAURIA

▲ *A family tree shows how the major dinosaur groups were related. The colored bands show how far back the fossil evidence for each group goes and tell us when these dinosaurs lived.*

CLASSIFYING DINOSAURS

Scientists classify dinosaurs by deciding how closely they are related to each other. For example, *Tyrannosaurus rex* belonged to the order Saurischia, with all other "lizard-hipped" dinosaurs. It was the suborder Theropoda, which includes all flesh-eating dinosaurs. Within that suborder it belonged to the infraorder Carnosauria. With other close relatives it formed the family Tyrannosauridae, or Tyrannosaurids. *Tyrannosaurus* is the name of its genus, and *rex* is its species name. Normally when we talk about a dinosaur we use the genus name.

dinosaurs included two-legged meat-eaters called **theropods** ("beast feet"), and four-legged plant-eaters called prosauropods and sauropods. Ornithischian dinosaurs were all plant-eaters. They included the two-legged ornithopods and pachycephalosaurs, and the four-legged stegosaurs, ankylosaurs, and ceratopsians.

Triassic times

The Age of Dinosaurs can be divided into three periods. The first of these was the **Triassic** (248 to 213 million years ago).

When the Triassic period began, most of the land was joined together as a single, mighty continent called **Pangaea** ("all earth"). But the supercontinent already showed signs of breaking up. A sea called the Tethys Ocean was beginning to open up between north and south. Geologists call northern Pangaea **Laurasia** and the south **Gondwana**.

Almost all of Laurasia and Gondwana was warm and dry. The ice that had covered parts of southern Pangaea in Permian times had melted. Winds could not carry moist sea air far inland, so great stretches of desert covered the countryside.

Nothing grew on the very driest land. But around the edges of the deserts seeds sprouted into cone-bearing trees that

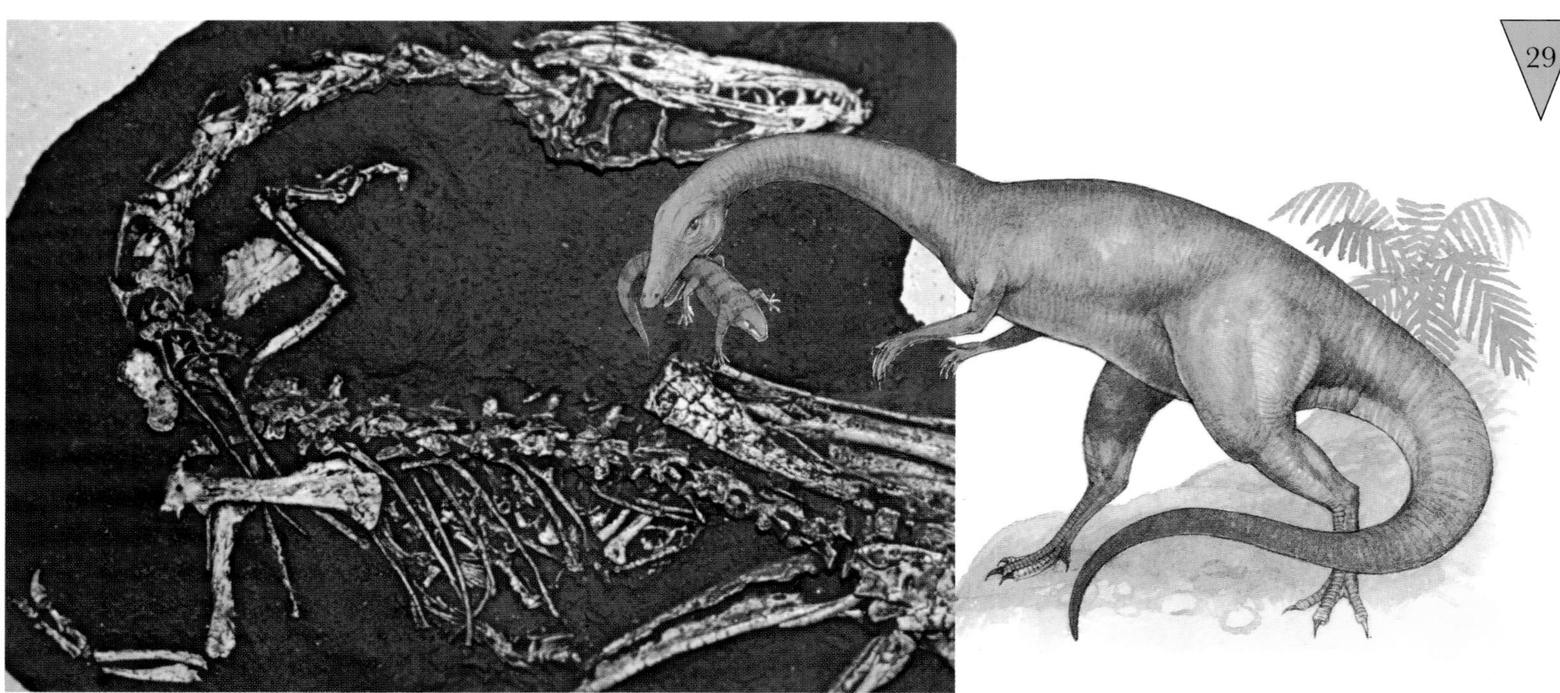

▲ *Coelophysis was a Triassic flesh-eating dinosaur. It grew up to 10 feet long, but was no heavier than a young child. This fossil skeleton of an adult contains the bones of a young* Coelophysis *that it had eaten, so it seems that* Coelophysis *may have been a cannibal.*

soared high into the light. There were also ginkgo trees much like those alive today. By pools and streams, where the soil was always damp, grew horsetails, ferns, and cycadeoids. There was no grass in the Age of Dinosaurs.

Triassic animals

New kinds of animals appeared on land, in the air, and in the sea during the Triassic period. Many were reptiles. Among these were pterosaurs with wings of skin that flew over seas where swam the first **ichthyosaurs** ("fish reptiles").

On land, there were heavy, armored thecodonts: some like crocodiles and others that ran on long hind limbs. They shared the land with other prehistoric creatures such as the first shrewlike mammals and the **rhynchosaurs** ("beaked reptiles"), strange tusked animals like pigs that rooted around for food. There were more familiar-looking creatures too: tortoises plodded, crocodiles hunted, lizards darted, frogs hopped, and salamanders wriggled across the landscape.

As the Triassic wore on, dinosaurs quickly came to replace the thecodonts. The first dinosaurs were sharp-toothed, two-legged hunters no bigger than a rabbit that could catch small reptiles in fingers armed with claws. From these small hunters came lightweight theropods: predators such as *Coelophysis* ("hollow form"), *Procompsognathus* ("before *Compsognathus*") and *Syntarsus* ("fused ankle"). At the same time, other, four-legged, saurischian dinosaurs evolved that ate leaves instead of meat. These prosauropods ("before the sauropods") had long necks and tails and bulky bodies. Early kinds, such as *Anchisaurus* ("near reptile"), grew little longer than a man. But *Plateosaurus* ("flat reptile") grew 26 feet long and *Melanorosaurus* ("black mountain reptile") half as long again.

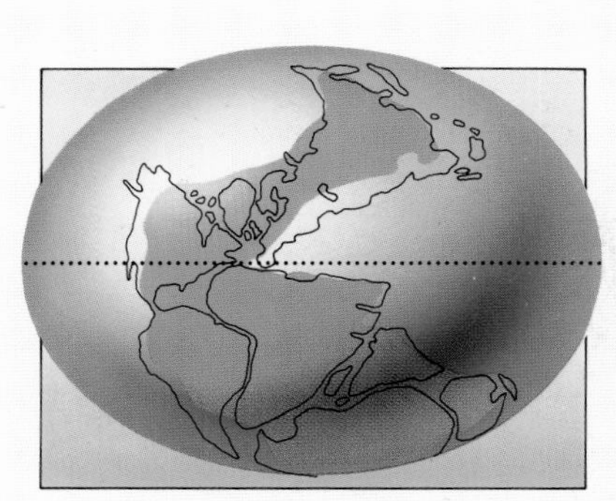

SHIFTING CONTINENTS

During the Triassic period the continents were joined together as one supercontinent called Pangaea. This allowed animals to spread across the world and explains why identical fossils of land animals have been found in places that are now miles apart.

By the end of the Triassic period, dinosaurs had spread across the whole of the supercontinent. They were to dominate the land for the next 150 million years.

The Jurassic period

The biggest dinosaurs lived in the **Jurassic period** (213 to 144 million years ago), the second period of the Mesozoic era.

During the Jurassic there were many changes to the earth's crust as the supercontinent Pangaea slowly split apart. Shallow seas spread over the parts of what are now North America and Europe. But in spite of all these changes, it would still have been possible to cross the world without getting wet feet!

Most places across the earth had a mild climate throughout the Jurassic period. Damp sea breezes now brought rain to deserts lying far inland. The rain fed rivers and these moistened the soil. Forests sprang up on the river banks.

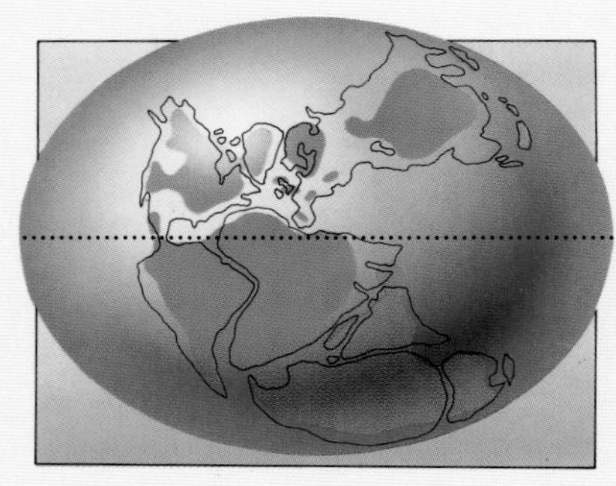

SHIFTING CONTINENTS

In the Jurassic Period the supercontinent Pangaea began to split up. There was still a large continent in the south, which geologists call Gondwana, but the northern land mass, Laurasia, had begun to break up into separate continents.

Jurassic animals

The dinosaurs of the Jurassic period were better equipped for killing prey or chewing and digesting leaves than their Triassic ancestors. New kinds of dinosaur also appeared at this time. The best known dinosaurs lived in what is now the United States. Here roamed the sharp-fanged hunter *Allosaurus* ("different reptile") and small, speedy predators such as *Ornitholestes* ("bird robber"). *Ornitholestes* probably ate lizards and *Allosaurus*'s leftovers. *Allosaurus* hunted large plant-eaters. Among these were huge, four-footed, long-necked sauropods ("reptile feet"), descended from the prosauropods. These included *Camarasaurus* ("chambered reptile"), *Apatosaurus* ("deceptive reptile"), and *Diplodocus* ("double beam"). *Brachiosaurus* ("arm reptile"), one of the largest sauropods, was taller than a house and as heavy as a herd of elephants.

There were big bird-hipped plant-eaters too. All had beaks and cheek teeth designed for eating leaves. A hungry *Allosaurus* might have made a meal of *Camptosaurus* ("bent reptile"), but spiky-tailed *Stegosaurus* ("roof reptile"), with its protective armor plating, would have been harder to tackle.

No land animals matched the dinosaurs for size. Jurassic mammals were mostly small, timid, mouselike creatures. Through the air flew pterosaurs and early birds with teeth, while crocodiles with flippers shared the shallow seas with ichthyosaurs and **plesiosaurs** ("near reptiles").

The Cretaceous period

This final and longest period of the Age of Dinosaurs lasted from 144 to 65 million years ago.

Shifting lands and rising sea levels reshaped the world during this time. Shallow seas spread across the northern lands

► *Living cycads produce big, leafy crowns and pine-like cones. Cycads resemble the stumpy, branchless cycadeoids that grew in the warm, wet Jurassic forests.*

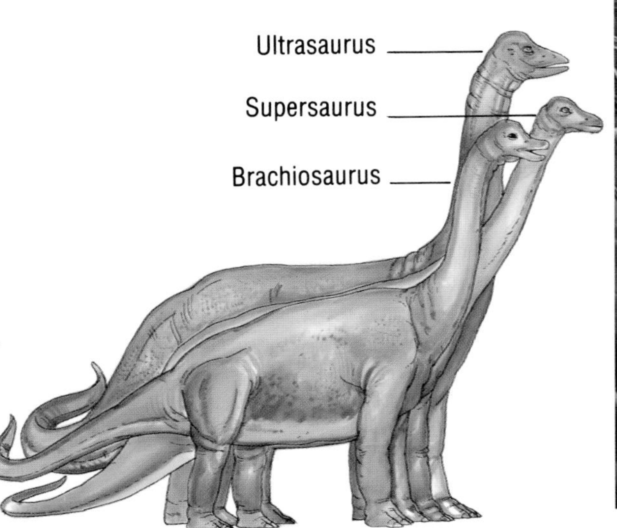

▲ *These three Jurassic giants were among the largest or longest dinosaurs of all time.* Brachiosaurus *is the biggest well known dinosaur. It stood up to 40 feet high and weighed 50 tons. Fossil bones belonging to* Supersaurus *and* Ultrasaurus, *however, suggest that these two monsters stood even taller.*

and the continents continued to drift apart. By the end of the Age of Dinosaurs, the earth looked almost as it does today. Where plates of the earth's crust collided, new rows of mountains in western North America were forced up. Later collisions would push up the Rocky Mountains, the Alps, and the great Himalayas.

▼ *A big, flesh-eating* Allosaurus *chases a small* Ornitholestes *in Late Jurassic times. Plant-eating dinosaurs browse peacefully in the distance.*

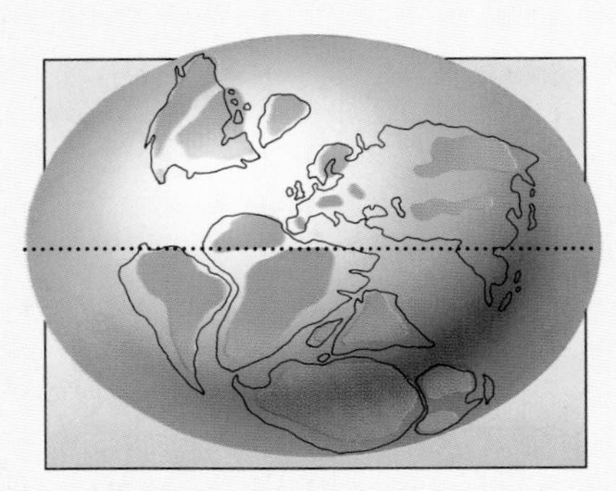

SHIFTING CONTINENTS

The continents continued to drift apart during the Cretaceous period. South America broke away from Africa and the Atlantic Ocean grew wider. Seas still covered what is now Europe. By the end of this period, the earth looked much as it does today.

▼ *These plant-eating dinosaurs and the tortoise lived in Early Cretaceous England.* Iguanodon *and the long-necked sauropods could browse on tree leaves. But* Hypsilophodon *and* Hylaeosaurus *could only reach low-growing vegetation.*

Iguanodon

Hypsilophodon

Although the climate was still mostly warm or mild during the **Cretaceous period**, winters could be chilly in the far north and south and on high mountain peaks.

New flowering plants began to spread, but the cycadeoids were dying out. The plant-eating animals that became most plentiful would have been those with teeth and stomachs that could cope best with this change in vegetation.

Cretaceous animals

There were more kinds of dinosaurs during the Cretaceous period than at any other time.

Lightweight hunters included dinosaurs such as *Ornithomimus* ("bird mimic") and *Struthiomimus* ("ostrich mimic"). Sharp-toothed predators with slashing claws, such as *Deinonychus* ("terrible claw"), *Troodon* ("wounding tooth"), and *Velociraptor* ("quick plunderer"), preyed on harmless plant-eating dinosaurs. But the biggest flesh-eating animals of all were the Late Cretaceous theropods *Tyrannosaurus* ("tyrant reptile") and *Spinosaurus* ("thorn reptile").

During the Cretaceous period, the sauropods grew scarcer. They were replaced by new, plant-eating ornithischian dinosaurs. Two-legged kinds ranged from little *Hypsilophodon* ("high ridge tooth") and *Dryosaurus* ("oak reptile") to the great duckbills *Edmontosaurus* ("Edmonton reptile") and *Parasaurolophus* ("beside *Saurolophus*"). There were plenty of four-legged ornithischians too. Tanklike ankylosaurs ("fused reptiles") included *Hylaeosaurus* ("woodland reptile") and *Silvisaurus* ("forest reptile"). Both were as long as a car.

▲ *New dinosaur discoveries are being made all the time.* Baryonyx walkeri *was uncovered in 1983 by William Walker and was officially named in 1986.* Baryonyx *roamed what is now southern England 124 million years ago. It may have used its long, curved claws to catch fish.*

Acanthopholis ("thorn bearer"), *Nodosaurus* ("node reptile") and *Ankylosaurus* ("fused reptile") were even bigger. Ceratopsians ("horned faces") outnumbered ankylosaurs. Small, two-legged ancestors such as *Psittacosaurus* ("parrot reptile") led to four-legged beasts with large heads such as *Protoceratops* ("first horned face"). From these came *Pentaceratops* ("five-horned face"), *Styracosaurus* ("spiked reptile"), and *Triceratops* ("three-horned face"), the biggest horned dinosaur of all.

These dinosaurs shared their world with the ancestors of modern water birds and mammals and the world's first snakes. Huge pterosaurs soared overhead. Plesiosaurs with snakelike necks and lizards with flipper-shaped limbs ruled the seas. But as the Cretaceous period drew to a close, so did the Age of Dinosaurs.

TYRANNOSAURUS REX

Tyrannosaurus rex, whose name means "king of the tyrant reptiles," was the largest ever flesh-eating dinosaur. Measuring 40 feet long and 18 feet tall, this huge predator weighed 6.4 tons. Its head alone measured 4 feet long and its jaws were lined with teeth that grew up to 7 inches long.

Hylaeosaurus

gentle giants

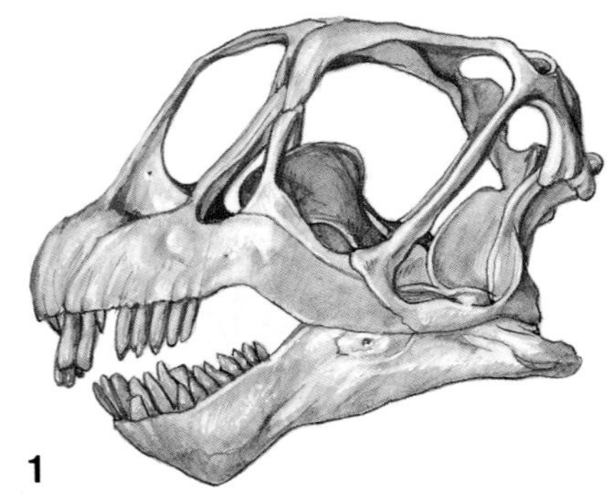

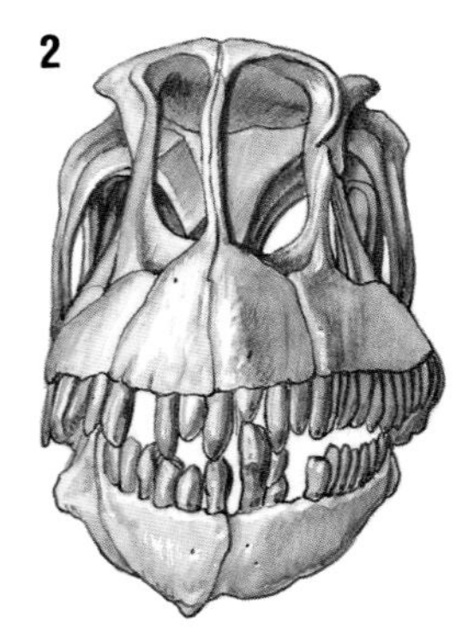

▲ Camarasaurus's *skull is shown here from the side (1) and the front (2). For such a huge animal the skull seems surprisingly small and fragile. Solid bone strengthens the jaws and covers the brain. But between the jaws and braincase there are big windows supported only by bony struts. Sockets in the dinosaur's skull show that* Camarasaurus *had large eyes and nostrils. Inside the skull was a brain that was little longer than a man's foot. For their body size, sauropods had smaller brains than any other backboned animals.*

The largest animals that ever lived on land were the sauropods, or "reptile feet." They get their name from their five-toed feet, which resemble those of a reptile. Most of these huge creatures looked like enormous elephants with long necks and tails. In fact, a big sauropod weighed more than several elephants put together. Because of their huge size, sauropods must have looked quite terrifying. In reality, however, they were harmless plant-eating creatures that spent their lives quietly feeding.

Sauropod ancestors

The sauropods were descended from animals called prosauropods ("before the sauropods"). These creatures roamed the world during the Late Triassic and Early Jurrasic periods and were among the first dinosaurs to eat plants. Four-legged *Anchisaurus* was a relatively small, lightly built creature measuring no more than 10 feet. Other prosauropods, such as *Lufengosaurus* ("Lufeng reptile"), grew about 20 feet long and could rear up on their hind legs to reach the leaves on high branches. *Melanorosaurus* was a much bigger, bulkier prosauropod that walked on all fours. The huge sauropods that appeared in the Late Jurassic were built along similar lines.

"Whale reptiles"

One of the earliest sauropods was *Cetiosaurus* ("whale reptile"). Fossils of its backbone were uncovered in England in the 1840s. At first scientists wrongly believed that these bones must have come from a colossal creature that had spent its life swimming in water, just as whales do now. This is how *Cetiosaurus* got its name. This enormous sauropod grew as long as five small cars and weighed as much as three elephants. It had a heavy backbone, unlike many of the later sauropods, and

► *This* Apatosaurus *gazes keenly around while it eats. The nervous monster must be always on the watch for an attack. Its size and thick, tough skin protect it from small theropods, but old scars on its back show where big flesh-eaters once pounced and tore out chunks of flesh. With luck and care a sauropod might live 200 years.*

teeth like flattened spoons for cropping leaves. Another early cetiosaurid, the Chinese *Shunosaurus* ("Shuo reptile"), is unusual as it is the first known sauropod with a bony club and short spikes on the end of its tail. A tail like that could have given enemies a nasty swipe if *Shunosaurus* was ever attacked.

▼ Diplodocus*'s skull was long and flattened with peglike teeth. It contained a brain no bigger than a cat's. Other diplodocids had long, low skulls very much like this.*

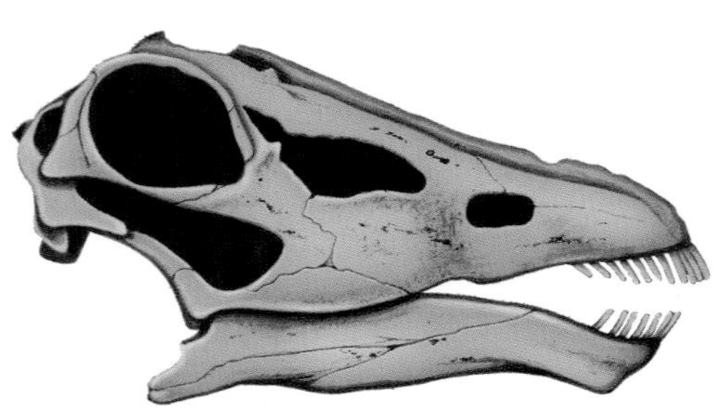

"Double beams"

Diplodocids ("double beams") get their names from their tail bones. These each had a piece of bone that stuck out forward and backward and supported the muscles that allowed the creatures to swing their tails. Diplodocids included immensely long, but surprisingly light, sauropods. One of the longest of all was *Diplodocus*. Measuring up to 88 feet from snout to tail tip, this beast was as long as a tennis court. More recent, but incomplete, fossil finds suggest that other dino-

DIPLODOCUS

A *Diplodocus* wallows in a Jurassic swamp as it feeds. At one time scientists argued that sauropods as big as *Diplodocus* must have lived permanently in lakes as they would not have been able to support their own weight on land. Another theory suggested that *Diplodocus* sprawled along the ground like an alligator. Scientists today know that this would have been impossible because the animal's huge ribcage would have gouged a great trench in the ground as it crept along. Experts now agree that *Diplodocus* stood upright and that its strong, pillar-like legs were perfectly able to support its body weight. This huge dinosaur may even have been able to rear up on its hind legs to reach tender leaves high up in the trees.

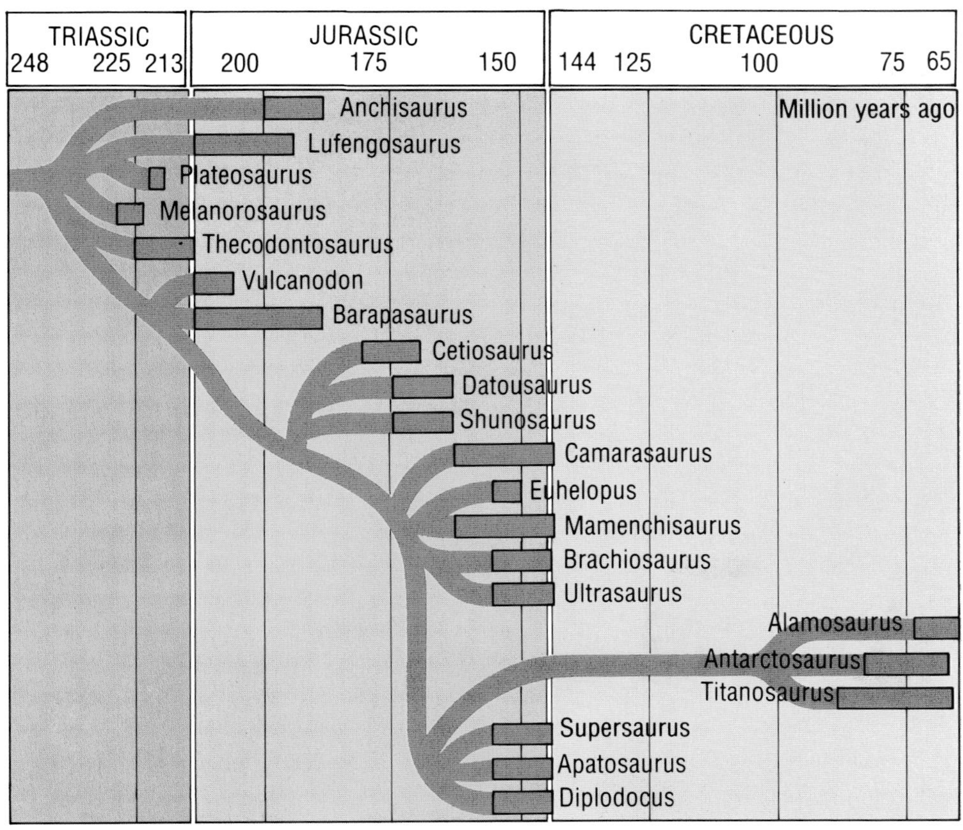

◀ *This family tree shows when various prosauropods and sauropods lived and how they were related. Lines that branch off close together from the same stem link dinosaurs that are thought to belong to the same family.* Thecodontosaurus *was a prosauropod that walked on two legs and only grew about 6 feet long.* Melanorosaurus, *on the other hand, was one of the biggest prosauropods. From animals such as these came early sauropods such as* Vulcanodon *and* Barapasaurus *that still showed some prosauropod features.* Euhelopus *and* Mamenchisaurus *both had extremely long necks. In fact,* Mamenchisaurus *had possibly the longest neck of any animal that has ever lived.*

saurs, such as *Supersaurus* ("super reptile"), may have been longer than *Diplodocus*, but this huge beast remains the longest well known dinosaur. Most of *Diplodocus*'s length was due to its snaky neck and whiplike tail. This is why it was lighter than other big dinosaurs, including its relative *Apatosaurus*. A scientist renamed that sauropod *Brontosaurus* ("thunder reptile"), because he thought its heavy feet thumped the ground with sounds like thunder. But its proper name is still *Apatosaurus*.

"Chambered reptiles"

Camarasaurus ("chambered reptile") gets its name from the hollows, or chambers, in its backbone. These hollows helped to lessen the weight of the animal's huge skeleton. Compared to most other sauropods, *Camarasaurus* had a relatively short neck and bigger, stronger teeth. *Camarasaurus* was the most widespread sauropod in Late Jurassic North America.

"Arm reptiles"

Brachiosaurus ("arm reptile") looked like an enormous giraffe as its front limbs were longer than its hind limbs. This huge creature was the largest, heaviest, and tallest of all well known dinosaurs. A big male *Brachiosaurus* grew about 80 feet long, towered 40 feet high and weighed about 50 tons. In 1979, however, the discovery of an incomplete skeleton suggested that an even bigger brachiosaurus existed. *Ultrasaurus* ("ultra reptile") possibly grew up to 55 feet tall, 82 feet long and may have weighed as much as 55 tons.

SAUROPOD RECORDS

The sauropods included the biggest land animals of all time. Below is a list of some sauropod record breakers. Many of these figures are estimates as fossil skeletons are often incomplete. New discoveries are being made all the time and may also alter this information.

The Longest Sauropods
(length in feet)

Supersaurus:	138
Unnamed titanosaurid:	115
Diplodocus:	88
Ultrasaurus:	82
Brachiosaurus:	72-82

The Tallest Sauropods
(height in feet)

Ultrasaurus:	52-56
Supersaurus:	50
Unnamed titanosaurid:	*46*
Brachiosaurus:	40

The Heaviest Sauropods
(weight in tons)

Unnamed titanosaurid:	*60-80*
Ultrasaurus:	45-55
Brachiosaurus:	50
Supersaurus:	40-50

▲ *The raised arm of a tall man would not have come up to the knee of a* Brachiosaurus, *one of the largest dinosaurs of all. Beasts this big could have squashed a person flat and barely noticed. Luckily, sauropods died out 60 million years before our apelike ancestors appeared.*

▼ *Some of the prosauropods and sauropods are pictured here in relation to man. Prosauropods such as* Lufengosaurus *and* Melanorosaurus *seem quite small compared to monsters such as* Brachiosaurus *and* Apatosaurus, *but* Melanorosaurus *was as long as seven men lying end to end.*

"Titanic reptiles"

Titanosaurids ("titanic reptiles") were sauropods with sloping heads and whiplike tails. The largest titanosaurid may have grown as long as 115 feet, but others were quite small, reaching a length of only 30 feet. Some titanosaurids had bony plates and studs set into their skin to protect their back and sides. Although most of the sauropods had died out before the end of the Cretaceous, one titanosaurid, *Alamosaurus* ("Alamo reptile"), is believed to have lived right up until 65 million years ago. If this is the case, *Alamosaurus* would have been the last sauropod of any kind.

The body of a giant

Sauropods came in various sizes, but they were all built along the same lines. Four limbs like pillars propped up a heavy, bulky body. At one end, a long neck supported a small head, while from the other end sprouted a long tail. A skeleton of bony "girders" protected the body's soft parts.

Long hind limb bones and massive hip bones carried most of a sauropod's weight, so these bones had to be strong and solid. The front limbs were usually shorter than the hind limbs, with massive shoulder blades that were sometimes as big as a man. Huge muscles joined the limb bones to the hip bones and shoulder blades and worked the heavy legs and arms.

A sauropod's backbone had to be strong in order to support its enormous body, but it also had to be light, otherwise it would have made the creature too heavy. So in most sauropods the bones of the backbone were hollowed out to save weight. The middle of the backbone supported the shoulders, the hips, and the huge, curved ribs which protected the heart, lungs, and intestines. The backbone's front end supported the neck and head, while at the back, it ran down inside the tail. Long, bony spines stuck up from the backbone, and cords called ligaments ran through V-shaped dips in these spines. Muscles pulled these ligaments tight to raise the head and tail.

In comparison to its huge body, a sauropod's head was tiny and, bulk for bulk, the biggest sauropods had the smallest brains of any backboned animal. They had large eyes, and

nostrils that opened high up on their skulls, like an elephant's. Their jaws were fairly weak, with only a few teeth, shaped like pegs or flattened spoons, at the front of the jaw.

▲ *African elephants hold clues as to how the sauropods may have lived. Like elephants, sauropods had strong, pillarlike legs for walking on dry land and probably lived in herds for greater protection.*

In water or on land?

At one time, scientists believed that the sauropods wallowed in lakes and rivers. There the water would have helped support their enormous bodies. People thought that the sauropods' great weight would have crushed their own limbs if they lived on land. The sauropods' teeth also suggested that these creatures lived in water as they only seemed strong enough for eating soft water plants. A lake might also have provided a safe retreat from a hungry predator's fangs.

Modern scientists have thrown out most of these ideas. They realized that sauropods could not have walked in deep water as the water pressure would have crushed their lungs. They have also worked out that a sauropod's legs and stumpy, padded toes were quite strong enough to bear its weight on land. These monsters could have walked around as easily as elephants. Fossil footprints show that sauropods *could* swim – but so could some flesh-eaters. The sauropods would have poled themselves through the water with their legs, while the carnosaurs swam by kicking with their hind limbs. Sauropods were probably no safer in water than they were on land. They may have swum to cross a river, or rolled in wet mud to drown itchy parasites and stop their hides getting too dry, but these dinosaur giants walked, slept, and ate on dry land.

▼ *People once thought that some sauropods had trunks because their nostril openings were positioned high up on their faces, like an elephant's. Few scientists accept this idea today, however.*

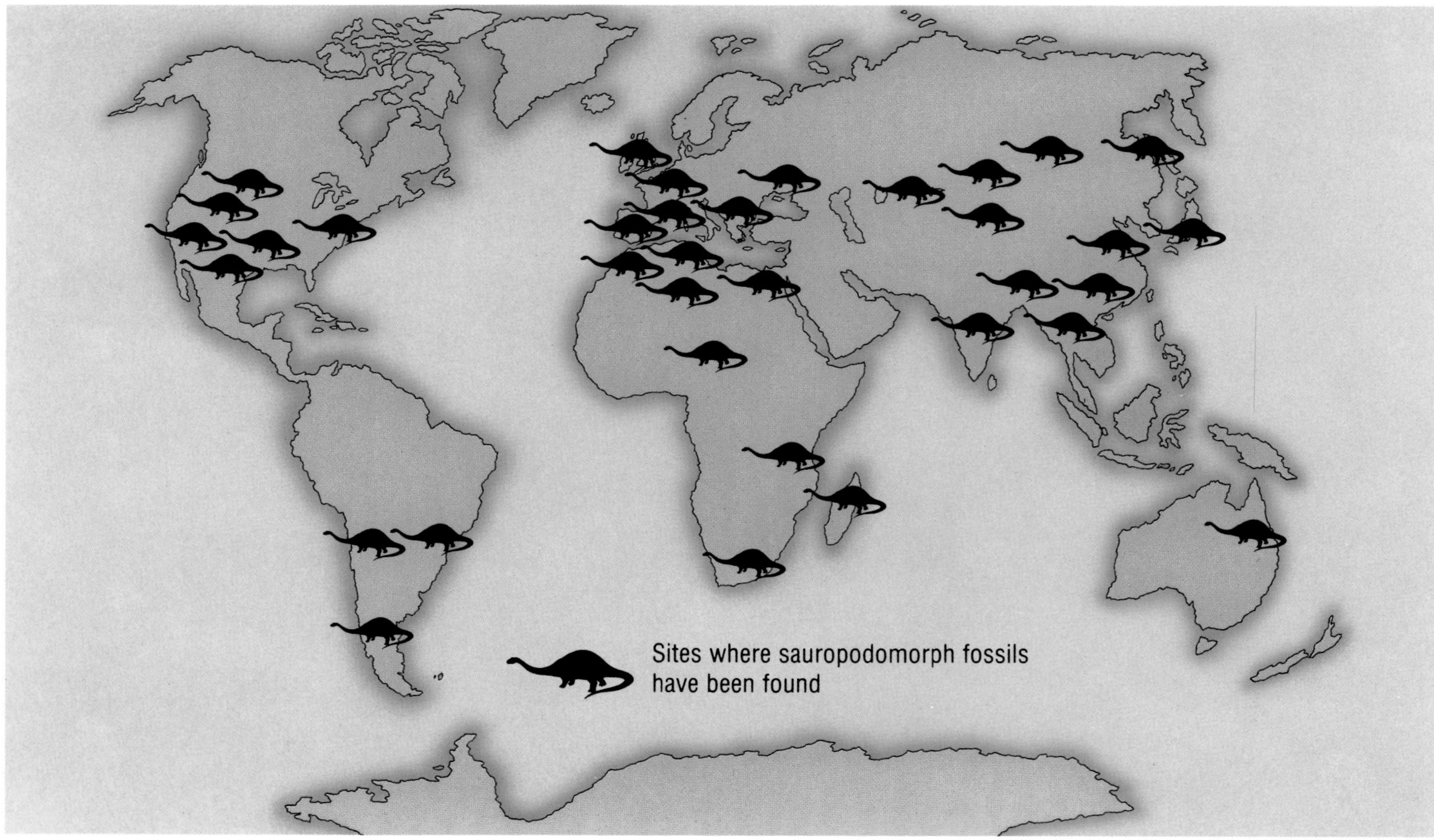

▲ *Fossil sauropods have been found on every continent except Antarctica. Cetiosaurids lived throughout the world. Brachiosaurids are known from all continents except South America. Titanosaurids lived everywhere except, perhaps, what is now Australia. Camarasaurid and diplodocid fossils come from everywhere except Australia and South America. Euhelopodid fossils only come from East Asia.*

SAUROPOD EGGS

In spite of the sauropods' huge size, their eggs were quite small. The biggest known sauropod egg was only 10-12 inches long and had an eggshell a tenth of an inch thick. This is probably as big as an egg could be. Big eggs need thick eggshells otherwise they will collapse. If a sauropod's egg had been bigger than 12 inches long, the shell would have been so thick that the young dinosaur would never have been able to break its way out!

What they ate

Scientists now believe that sauropods spent their days browsing on ferns and leaves that were too high for other dinosaurs to reach. Sauropods had no cheek teeth for chewing leaves. So in order to break down their plant food, they swallowed stones that ground the leaves to pulp inside their stomachs. When the stones wore down, the dinosaurs would have spat them out and swallowed more. We can only guess how much food they ate. If their bodies were warm-blooded like a mammal's, big sauropods would have had to crop a ton of leaves a day! It is hard to see how the creatures' narrow throats could have swallowed the food fast enough. They probably needed much less food than that, however, because their bodies used up energy more slowly than a mammal's would.

Sauropod wanderers

Fossil footprints found in Texas show where 23 sauropods passed by one day; similar tracks have been found elsewhere. These tracks seem to suggest that sauropods lived and roamed in herds, moving on in search of new feeding grounds once they had stripped all the leaves from one grove of trees.

As a herd walked along, its members would have kept a sharp lookout for any sign of danger. If a pack of hungry flesh-eaters appeared, the herd probably drew close together. Small, thin-skinned babies would have huddled in the middle with their mothers. Around them, huge, tough-skinned male

◀ Their long necks make this herd of sauropods look rather like a herd of giant giraffes. Only the tallest treetops stood out of reach and were safe from these browsing creatures. When the herd had eaten all the food in one area, it would have tramped off through the forest to find a new feeding ground, leaving well-worn paths to show where it had passed.

sauropods would have formed a living wall. If the predators attacked, these guards may have reared up and brought their forelimbs crashing down on the enemy. Sharp claws on their front feet may also have been used as defensive weapons, or they may have lashed out with their long, whiplike tails.

We can only guess how these dinosaur herds behaved. And we can only guess how sauropods produced their young. Discoveries of big fossil eggs hint that all sauropods hatched from eggs laid in the ground. Perhaps a mother left the herd to lay her eggs, then waited for the sun's heat to hatch them. When her eggs had hatched, the mother would somehow have led her babies back to the safety of the herd. Not all her babies would have lived to become adults, but those that did led strange and fascinating lives.

The end of the sauropods

By Late Jurassic times, thousands of sauropods roamed the forests that grew along the banks of lakes and rivers around the world. In time, however, new kinds of plants with tough leaves replaced those plants on which the sauropods fed. Perhaps these new plants proved just too tough for sauropods to eat. Certainly, big, new, bird-hipped dinosaurs appeared in the Cretaceous period that could chew more efficiently than the sauropods. While these new plant-eaters multiplied, the sauropods grew scarcer. Few sauropods were still around when all the dinosaurs became extinct.

▼ The footprints of a walking man are compared to those of a sauropod that left its tracks in mud 150 million years ago. The mud later hardened into rock, preserving the sauropod's footprints. The smaller sauropod prints were made by the animal's front limbs. Its hind limbs punched holes as big as washtubs. You can also see marks made by "thumb" claws and large claws on the first three toes.

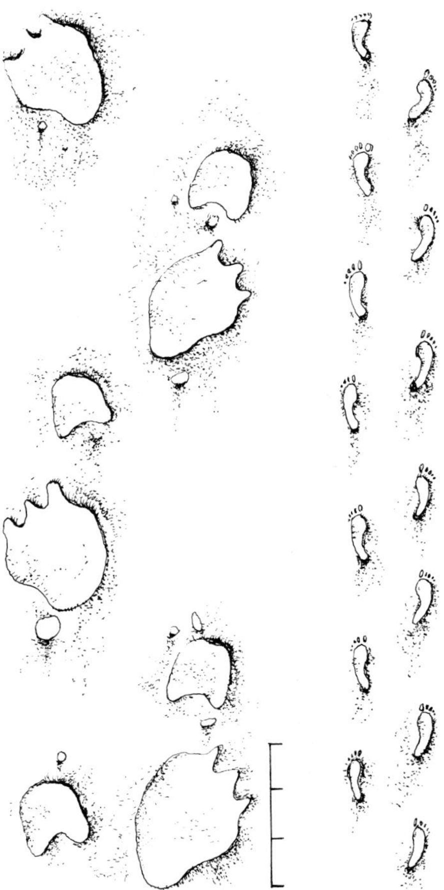

fearful fangs

When some people hear the word "dinosaur," they think of a huge, harmless, four-legged sauropod, but most of us imagine a fierce, two-legged flesh-eater such as *Tyrannosaurus*. *Tyrannosaurus* was one of the last of a long line of flesh-eating dinosaurs going back to the start of the Mesozoic era. These are called theropods, or "beast feet."

▲ *These damp, dark dips are a megalosaurid's footprints. They were formed when a big flesh-eating dinosaur walked across soft mud perhaps 150 million years ago. The well-preserved tracks suggest that megalosaurids walked with their toes turned in.*

The big flesh-eaters

Among the theropods were large dinosaurs that some people class together as "carnosaurs" ("meat reptiles"). These big flesh-eating dinosaurs lived all through the Age of Dinosaurs and included the largest ever hunters on land.

The fearsome creatures were built along broadly similar lines. They walked or ran on two strong hind legs. Their arms were much smaller than their legs, but their fingers were armed with sharp claws. A long, strong tail balanced a short, thick neck and massive head. Their jaws could gape wide, and bristled with sharp teeth.

"Giant reptiles"

Like other dinosaurs, the carnosaurs can be divided into related groups called families.

Megalosaurids, or "giant reptiles," were a dinosaur family that lived from Early Jurassic into Cretaceous times. The best known megalosaurid is *Megalosaurus*. This mighty hunter grew up to 30 feet long. It had huge legs with thick, solid bones

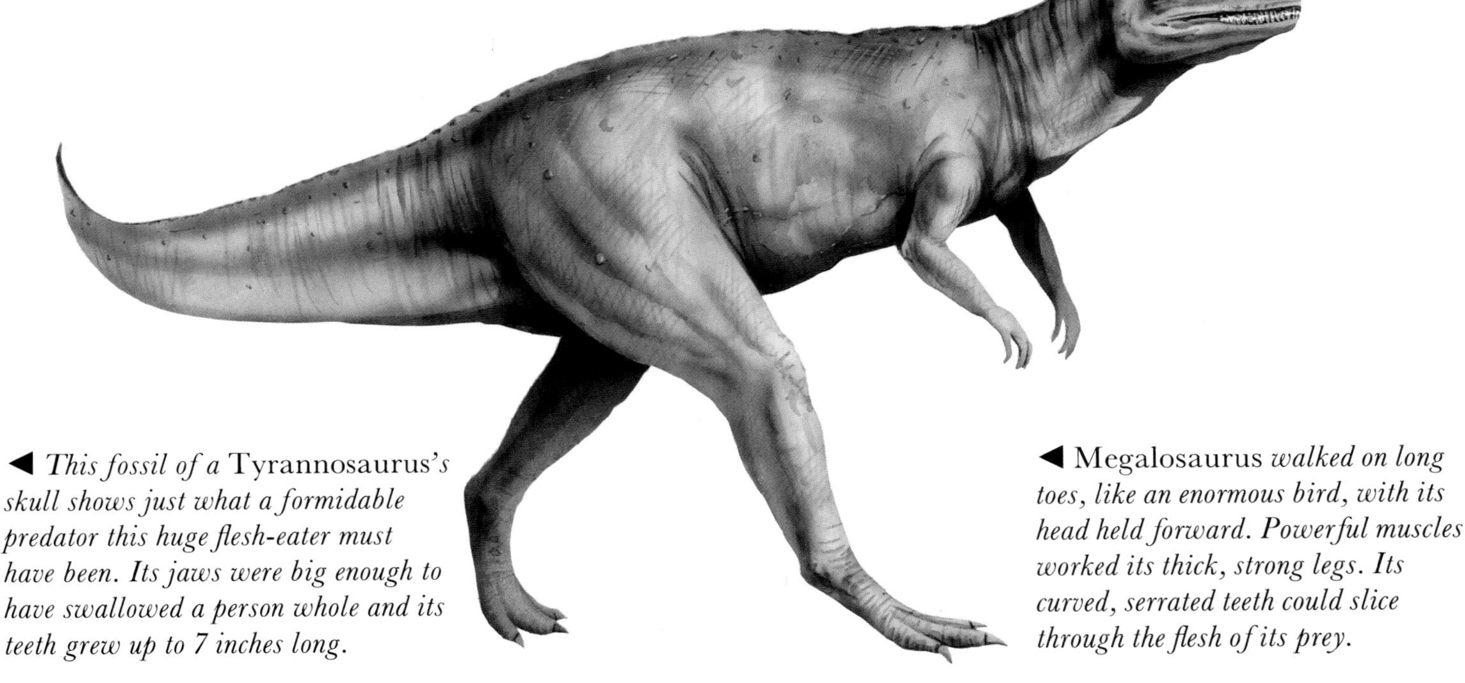

◀ *This fossil of a* Tyrannosaurus's *skull shows just what a formidable predator this huge flesh-eater must have been. Its jaws were big enough to have swallowed a person whole and its teeth grew up to 7 inches long.*

◀ Megalosaurus *walked on long toes, like an enormous bird, with its head held forward. Powerful muscles worked its thick, strong legs. Its curved, serrated teeth could slice through the flesh of its prey.*

▲ *The great flesh-eater* Spinosaurus *had a huge sail of skin on its back. A male* Spinosaurus *may have used this to scare off its male rivals. Or perhaps* Spinosaurus *used the sail to control its body temperature, standing sideways to the sun when it wanted to warm itself, and with its back to the sun when it needed to cool down.*

to support its long, strong body. Its prey were probably sauropods and stegosaurs, which it would have attacked using the sharp claws on its three fingers and its powerful jaws. These were lined with curved, saw-edged teeth that could have torn great chunks of flesh from its victim's side.

Unusual carnosaurs

Among the big flesh-eaters were some strangely shaped animals. Bony spines as tall as a man stuck up from the backbone of *Spinosaurus*. Scientists believe that they held up a web of skin rather like a sail. It is possible that *Spinosaurus* used this sail to control its body temperature. Another unusual carnosaur, *Carnotaurus* ("meat-eating bull"), had broad horns that stuck out sideways above its eyes.

Nightmare monsters

Among the biggest of all the theropods were the allosaurids ("different reptiles") and tyrannosaurids ("tyrant reptiles").

Allosaurus grew as long as a bus and was heavier than *Megalosaurus*. Its three-fingered hands had sharp, curved claws that *Allosaurus* would have used to grasp its prey and also to tear off the flesh from bones. Rows of serrated, bladelike fangs lined its huge jaws, which could have bitten great mouthfuls out of

▼ *A* Tyrannosaurus *stands over the half-eaten body of a hadrosaurid that it has killed.* Tyrannosaurus *may have been able to run as quickly as a horse to catch its prey.*

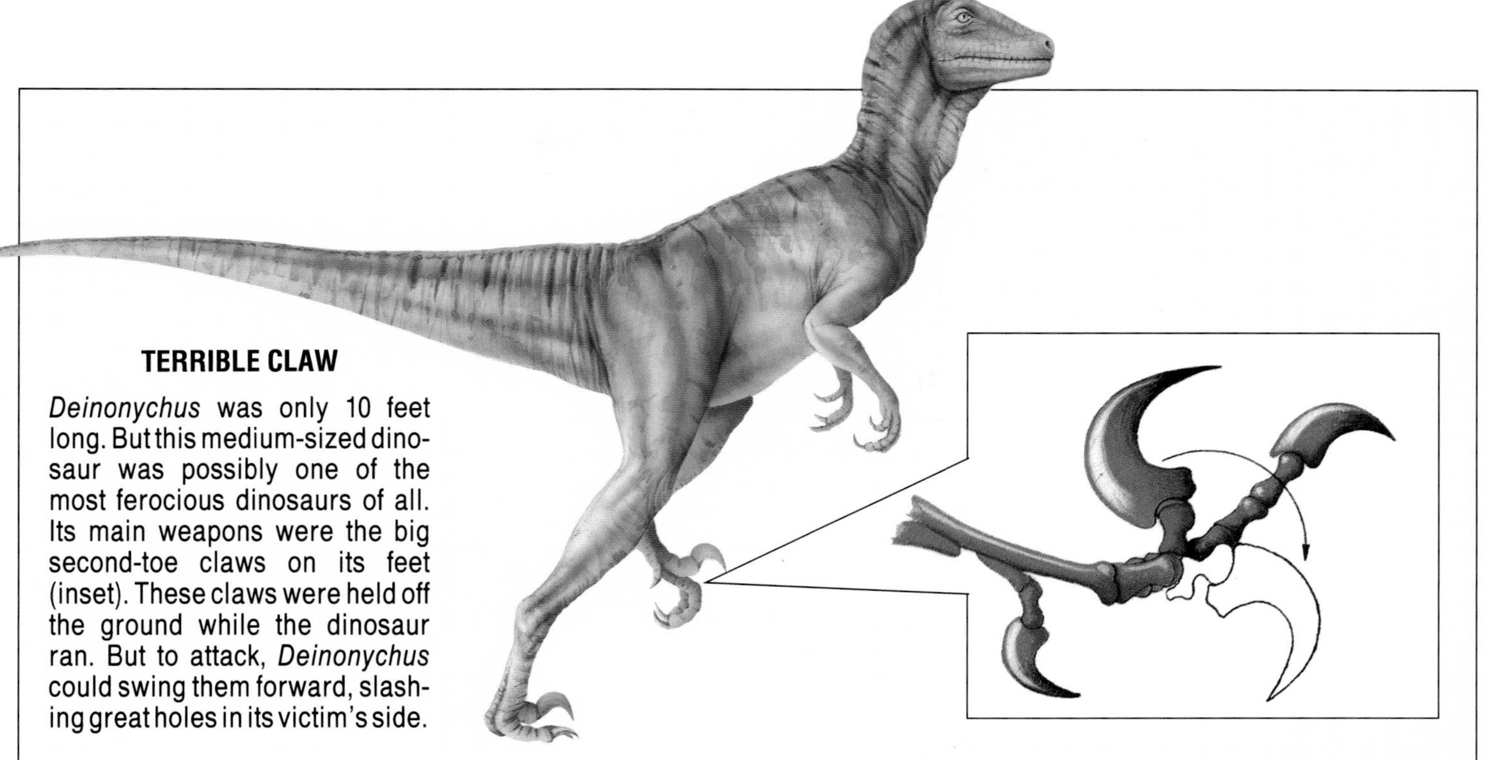

TERRIBLE CLAW

Deinonychus was only 10 feet long. But this medium-sized dinosaur was possibly one of the most ferocious dinosaurs of all. Its main weapons were the big second-toe claws on its feet (inset). These claws were held off the ground while the dinosaur ran. But to attack, *Deinonychus* could swing them forward, slashing great holes in its victim's side.

its victim. It is quite likely that *Allosaurus* hunted in packs, just as wolves do today. Working together, a pack of *Allosaurus* could have brought down sauropods that were sometimes more than twice their size.

Much later, an even more terrifying dinosaur appeared. *Tyrannosaurus* was probably the biggest, heaviest carnosaur of all. This monster grew 40 feet long and weighed more than most big elephants. If it were alive today, *Tyrannosaurus* could have reared up to peer into an upstairs window. Usually, however, it walked with its head held low and forward, and its heavy tail held out behind for balance. One of the most curious things about *Tyrannosaurus* was its tiny arms. They were far too short to use to shovel food into its mouth, or even to seize prey. In order to catch its food, *Tyrannosaurus* may have charged its victim head first with jaws open wide to take great bites out of its side. An extra hinge in its jaw allowed *Tyrannosaurus* to open its mouth wide enough to do this.

▼ *This fossil tooth of a large flesh-eater dates back to Late Jurassic times. Its saw-toothed edges helped it to bite through flesh as easily as a steak knife cuts through a thick steak.*

Terrible claws

Not all the fiercest dinosaurs were big. The ferocious hunters called deinonychosaurs ("terrible claw reptiles") were little larger than a man. But dinosaurs such as *Deinonychus* and *Velociraptor* were powerfully armed. They had long legs and a sharp second-toe claw that flicked forward for attack and could inflict terrible wounds. Like *Allosaurus*, these fearsome flesh-eaters may also have hunted in packs. A pack of *Deinonychus* could have cornered and killed a dinosaur almost as big as an elephant. Each hunter would have stood on one foot, balanced by its long, stiff tail. As it bit and grappled, it could strike out with its other foot and rip open its victim's belly. *Deinonychus* was perhaps the fiercest dinosaur of all.

▼ *Fossil bones found in Mongolia's Gobi Desert show the deinonychosaur* Velociraptor *still gripping the head shield of its victim, the plant-eating* Protoceratops. *The hunter was using its sharp toe claws to wound its prey, while the* Protoceratops *seems to have crashed its armored head through the* Velociraptor*'s chest. Nobody knows why both dinosaurs died together. Perhaps they died from their injuries while they were still locked together. Or maybe they were suffocated by a sudden sandstorm.*

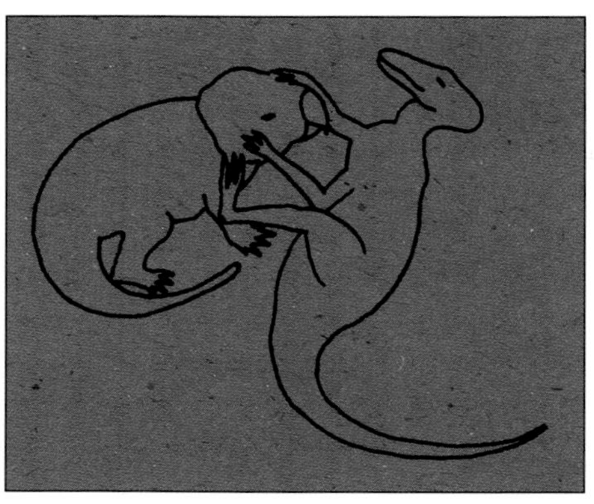

An unsolved mystery

In 1979, a new dinosaur was named *Segnosaurus*, or "slow reptile." Although many scientists classify this unusual dinosaur as a theropod, *Segnosaurus* does not show all the theropod characteristics. Like other flesh-eaters, it had short arms that ended in three clawed fingers. But instead of having a mouth full of sharp, daggerlike teeth, *Segnosaurus* appears to have had a horny beak with small, pointed teeth at the back of its jaw. Some people think that *Segnosaurus* hunted fish, but this still does not explain why it had a horny beak. Scientists are still puzzling over this mysterious dinosaur.

"Hollow-tailed reptiles"

Alongside the carnosaurs and the fierce deinonychosaurs lived several groups of small flesh-eaters. Some people class these all together under the term "coelurosaurs" ("hollow-tailed reptiles") for convenience. While the carnosaurs were big and heavy, the coelurosaurs were mostly small and light. Whereas carnosaurs had solid bones to bear their weight, coelurosaurs' bones were thin and hollow. Coelurosaurs were more agile than the carnosaurs; most hunted animals no bigger than a lizard or a mouse.

About 15 kinds of these small predators formed the family called the coelurids. These creatures had slim, low heads and narrow jaws crammed with small, sharp teeth. The head and

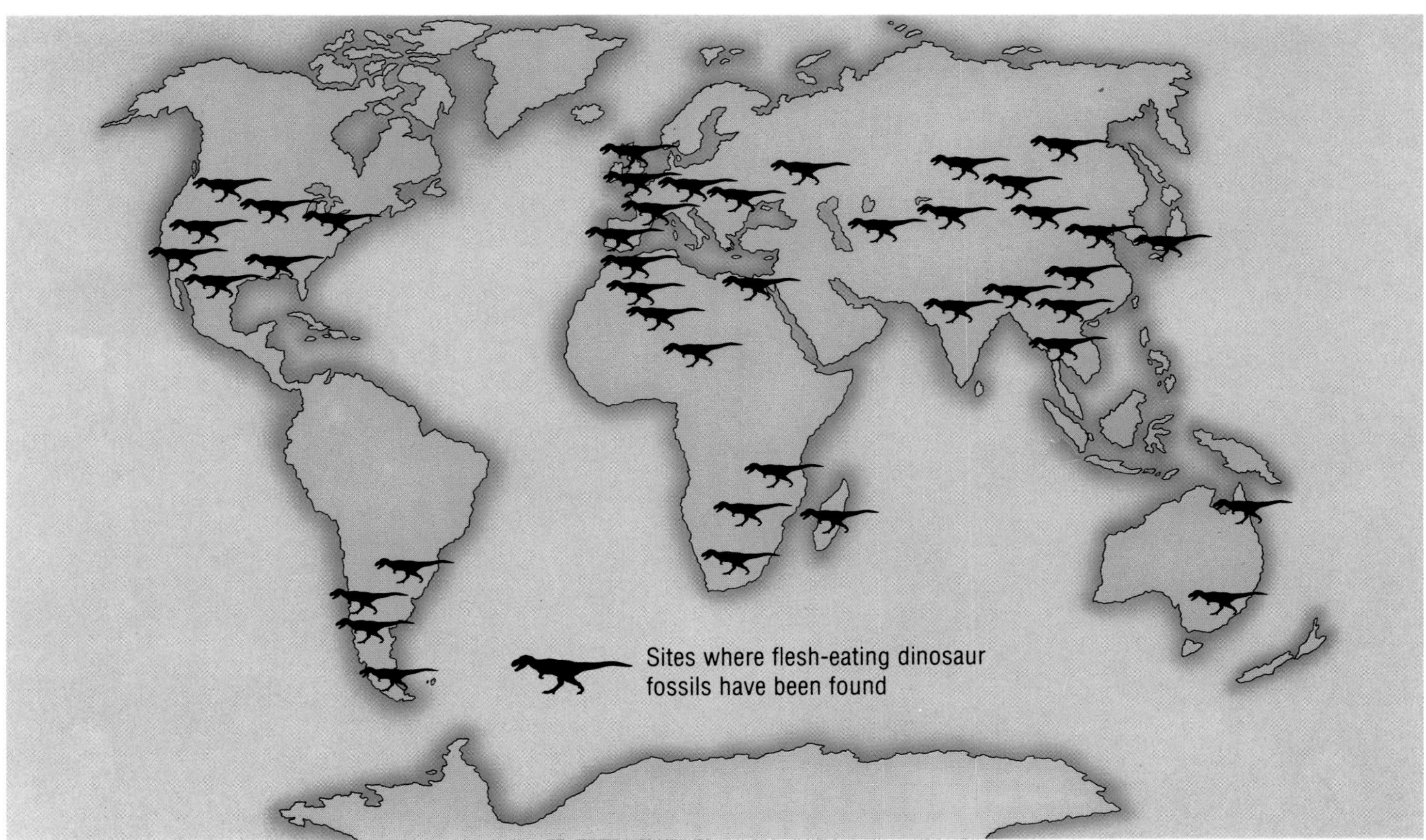

long neck were balanced by an even longer tail, while the strong, slender hind limbs suggest that the coelurids could run quite quickly. These dinosaurs' arms were shorter than their legs and ended in three fingers that were tipped with sharp, curved claws.

Ornitholestes ("bird robber") was among the largest of the coelurids. The scientist who named it thought it may have seized birds in its long, clawed hands. Like *Ornitholestes*, *Coelurus* ("hollow tail") was 6 feet long from nose to tail. Both *Ornitholestes* and *Coelurus* were lighter than a man and ran on their toes with their necks stretched forward. These slender hunters could dart through undergrowth that was too thick for carnosaurs. Their sharp eyes could search out lizards, mouse-like mammals, birds, or pterosaurs. Having spotted their prey, *Coelurus* and *Ornitholestes* would then seize it in their strong, curved claws before the startled creature had time to escape. Another possible source of food may have been the leftovers from a carnosaur's kill. Just as modern jackals eat the leftovers from a lion's kill, the coelurosaurs may have torn scraps of meat off carcasses when dinosaurs such as *Allosaurus* had had their fill.

Coelurosaurs included some of the smallest of all dinosaurs. *Compsognathus* ("pretty jaw") was little larger than a chicken and even looked much like a bird. But it had scaly skin, not feathers, arms instead of wings, and small, sharp teeth instead of a toothless beak. For food, *Compsognathus* probably chased after lizards on its long hind limbs.

▲ *Allosaurid fossils have been found everywhere except Antarctica. Megalosaurids and deinonychosaurs have been found in Europe, Asia, and North Africa. The tyrannosaurids' strongholds were what are now East Asia and North America. Ostrich dinosaurs lived there and also in what is now Africa. Small theropods roamed across the whole globe.*

▼ Segnosaurus *had broad hind feet unlike the birdlike feet of other theropods. They may even have been webbed for swimming.*

Compsognathus must have used up energy very quickly as it sprinted after its prey. Scientists believe it could keep active for quite a while, unlike a lizard, which loses energy and slows down fairly quickly. This suggests that *Compsognathus* and other hunting dinosaurs may have been warm-blooded. To stay active, however, *Compsognathus* would have had to keep its body warm. Scaly dinosaur skin trapped heat less well than fur or feathers and, size for size, small dinosaurs had much more skin for losing body heat than big carnosaurs. To solve this problem some small dinosaurs may have grown scales that frayed at the edges. If the split ends interlocked, they would have trapped warm air against the dinosaur's body and helped slow down the rate at which it cooled.

◀ Ornithomimus *(facing page) was one of a group of large birdlike dinosaurs. It may have pecked fruit from bushes with its toothless beak or eaten other dinosaurs' eggs. If attacked,* Ornithomimus *could sprint away as fast as an ostrich.*

THEROPOD RECORDS

Some record-breaking facts about the ferocious flesh-eaters:

The Largest Theropod
Tyrannosaurus: measured 40 feet long and weighed up to 6.4 tons

Longest Theropod
Spinosaurus: measured 50 feet long and weighed 4 tons

The Smallest Theropod
Saltopus: measured 2 feet long and may only have weighed 2 pounds

The Brainiest Theropod
Troodon: had the largest brain, for its size, of any known dinosaur

Birds from dinosaurs.

"Feathers" is the name we give to the frayed scales that grow on birds. Most scientists agree that birds evolved from feathered coelurosaurs, although no one knows for certain as feathers are so frail that few have survived as fossils. We do know, however, that early birds flew about on the warm desert islands where *Compsognathus* lived. Indeed, the bones of both are so alike that even experts have mistaken bird fossils for a fossil of that little dinosaur. If birds are dinosaurs with feathers, then they are the only descendants of the dinosaurs to have survived to modern times.

Ostrich dinosaurs

Like birds, some of the later hunting dinosaurs lost their teeth. In poor light these theropods would have looked very much like those big, flightless birds: ostriches and emus.

Imagine that a time machine could whisk you back to western North America 70 million years ago. It is late evening and you think you see an ostrich. The creature stands more than

▼ Compsognathus *and the bird-dinosaur* Archaeopteryx *would have looked amazingly alike seen side by side. The main difference was that* Archaeopteryx *had feathers.*

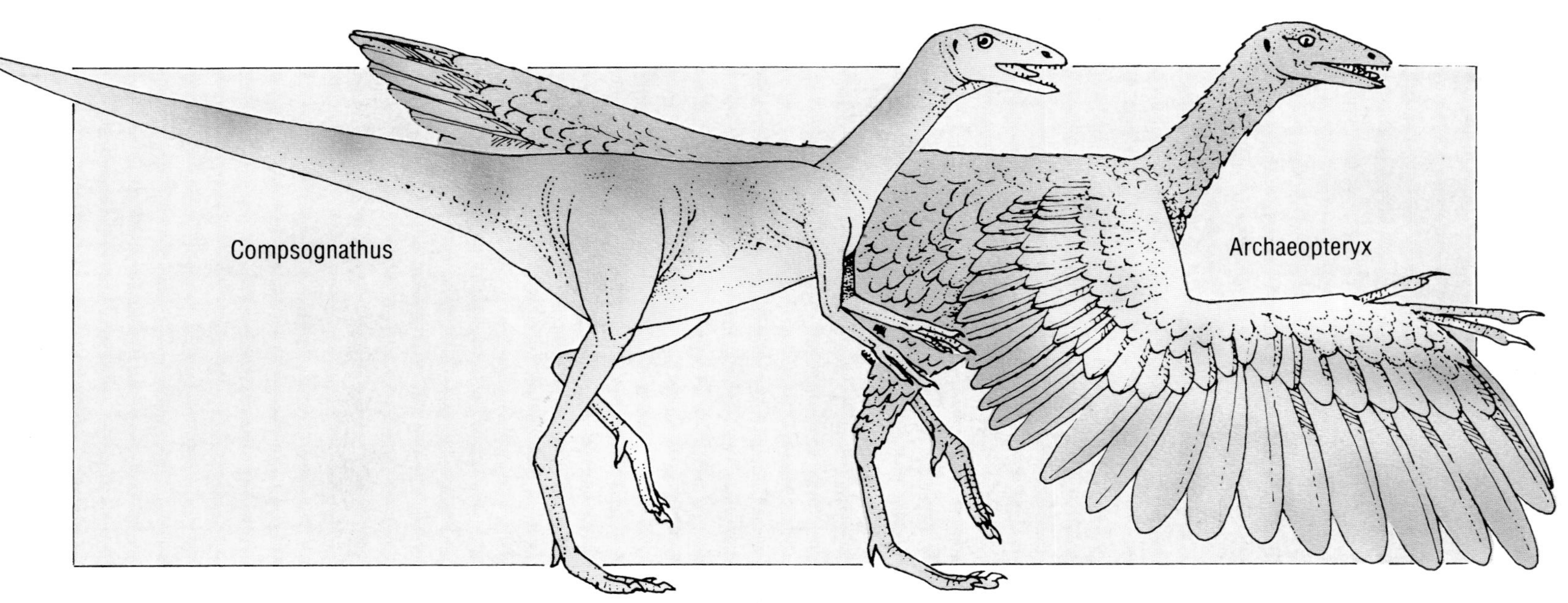

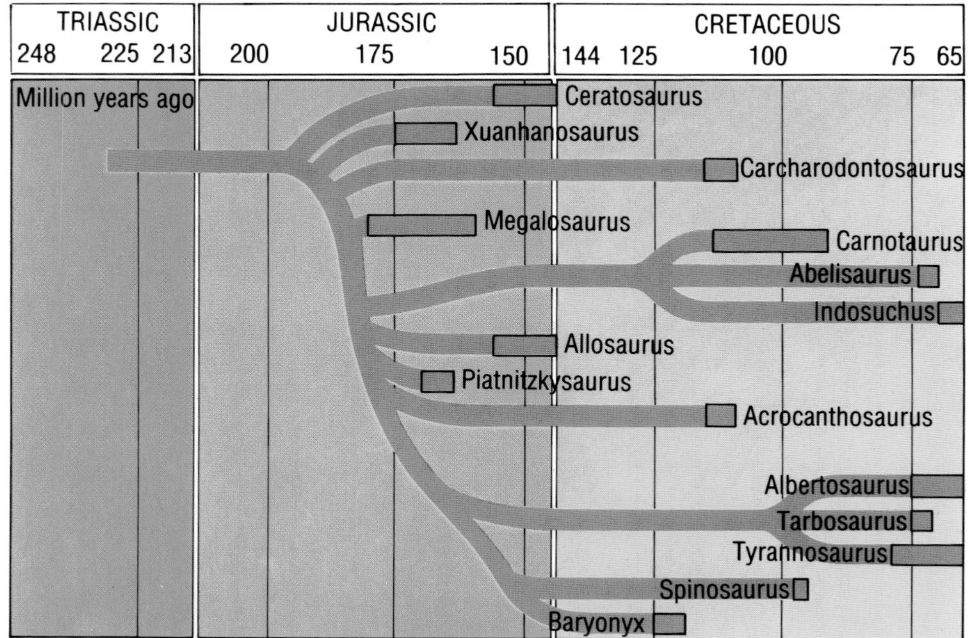

◀ *Scientists sometimes have to use guesswork when working out how the big flesh-eaters were related. This is because many are known only from a few teeth and one or two bones.* Ceratosaurus *is unusual because it had a horn on its nose. It may have used this to fight rival males for a mate. Scientists still do not know for certain how* Xuanhanosaurus, *a little known dinosaur from China, and* Carcharodontosaurus *fit in with the other big flesh-eaters. The two dinosaurs* Abelisaurus *and* Indosuchus *are known only from their skulls. Scientists think they were members of the same family as the horned* Carnotaurus. *Both* Piatnitzkysaurus *and* Acrocanthosaurus *were similar to* Allosaurus. Acrocanthosaurus *may also have had a small sail along its back.* Tarbosaurus *had an even longer skull than its relative* Tyrannosaurus.

6 feet high and walks on long, strong hind legs. It has a beak and big, keen eyes like an ostrich. But its skin is bare, not feathered, and it holds a stiff, naked tail off the ground to balance its long, bare neck. Instead of wings, it has arms with clawed hands. This is not an ostrich but an *Ornithomimus* ("bird mimic"), one of a group of strange theropods called ornithomimids.

We can only guess how these ostrich dinosaurs lived. Some scientists believe that they tore open ants' nests with their clawed fingers, then lapped up the ants with a long, sticky tongue. Others think that ornithomimids may have brushed away the sand covering other dinosaurs' eggs and sucked these dry. But the most likely suggestion is that they pecked at fruits and leaves, or chased flying insects and small reptiles such as lizards.

Ostrich dinosaurs could deliver a powerful kick with their hind limbs, but their best defense against a hungry enemy was a speedy getaway. Some could run as quickly as a racehorse to escape an attacking carnosaur.

More birdlike curiosities

Alongside the ostrich dinosaurs lived smaller toothless oddities. *Oviraptor* ("egg thief") and *Avimimus* ("bird mimic") looked rather like small ornithomimids. In certain ways, however, they were quite different. Whereas most ornithomimids had a long, narrow beak, at least some kinds of *Oviraptor* had a short, deep, toothless beak and a tall, bony crest. Just as odd were the two small bony points that these dinosaurs had in the roof of their mouths. The bony points could have been used to crush the dinosaur eggshells or snails' shells that some scientists believe were their main food. This is why they were given the name "egg thief."

▼ *A Late Jurassic seashore scene shows a hungry* Ornitholestes *chasing after a much smaller* Compsognathus. Archaeopteryx *flutters in the foreground.*

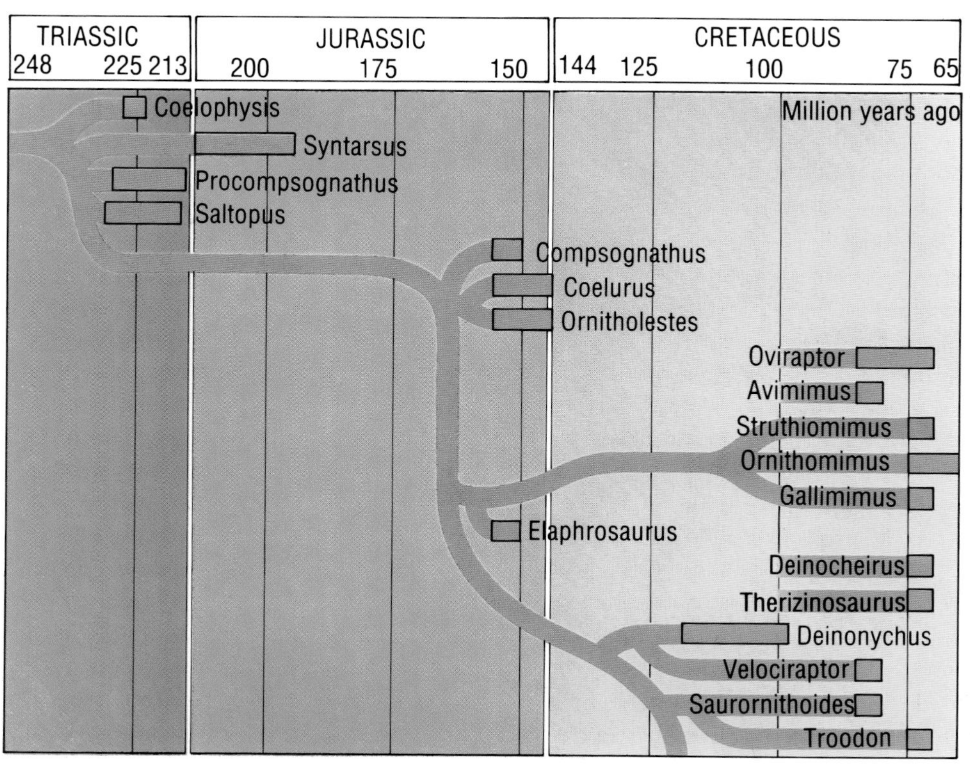

◀ *Small flesh-eaters were among the first dinosaurs to appear on the earth, but scientists are still unsure of how they were all related. Little* Saltopus *was only 2 feet long and could be one of the oldest dinosaurs in the world.* Elaphrosaurus *may have been an ancestor of ornithomimids such as* Struthiosaurus *and* Gallimimus. Deinocheirus *and* Therizonosaurus *both had very long arms measuring about 8 feet. Scientists are unsure how they fit in with other theropod families.* Saurornithoides, *a deinonychosaur similar to* Troodon, *had a large brain and was probably more intelligent than most dinosaurs.*

Avimimus had no such bony points, but its upper beak had a zigzag edge like a saw blade – good for gripping wriggling prey such as lizards, perhaps. Even more remarkable were its little arms, which folded back like a bird's wings. A long, bony ridge along one of the front limb bones also suggests that *Avimimus*'s arms and body may have been covered with feathers. If this is the case, *Avimimus* must have looked even more birdlike than an ostrich dinosaur.

bird-hipped bipeds

HYPSILOPHODON

Scientists once thought that *Hypsilophodon* perched in trees. Today, however, experts have realized that its toes could not have grasped the branches to climb up. Instead, they believe that *Hypsilophodon* lived on the ground, where its long foot bones would have allowed it to run away quickly from its enemies.

The bulky plant-eating sauropods and the more agile flesh-eaters were very different animals, but they shared one common feature: they were both saurischian, or "lizard-hipped," dinosaurs. Meanwhile, other dinosaurs called ornithischian, or "bird-hipped," dinosaurs had also evolved.

The ornithischian dinosaurs were plant-eaters and many walked and ran on their hind limbs like the theropods. Most of these bird-hipped bipeds belonged to a group called ornithopods, or "bird-feet." Ornithopods had no sharp claws or fangs with which to defend themselves from a hungry carnosaur. They relied on their size or on a speedy getaway for survival. When they ran, special bony rods in their tails helped to keep these off the ground to balance the front part of their bodies. The ornithopods lived on a diet of leafy plants. They had horny beaks that could snip off shoots and young branches and leaf-shaped cheek teeth designed for breaking down tough plant matter. Roomy cheek pouches could store food before the animals swallowed it.

► *From its skeleton we know that* Camptosaurus *could rear up on its hind limbs or go down on all fours. This dinosaur probably walked slowly on all fours much of the time, but would have stood on its hind limbs to browse on leafy trees.*

Small sprinters

The first bird-hipped bipeds were lively creatures no bigger than a dog. From ancestors such as little *Fabrosaurus* ("Fabre's reptile") came a long line of speedy sprinters that spread right across the world.

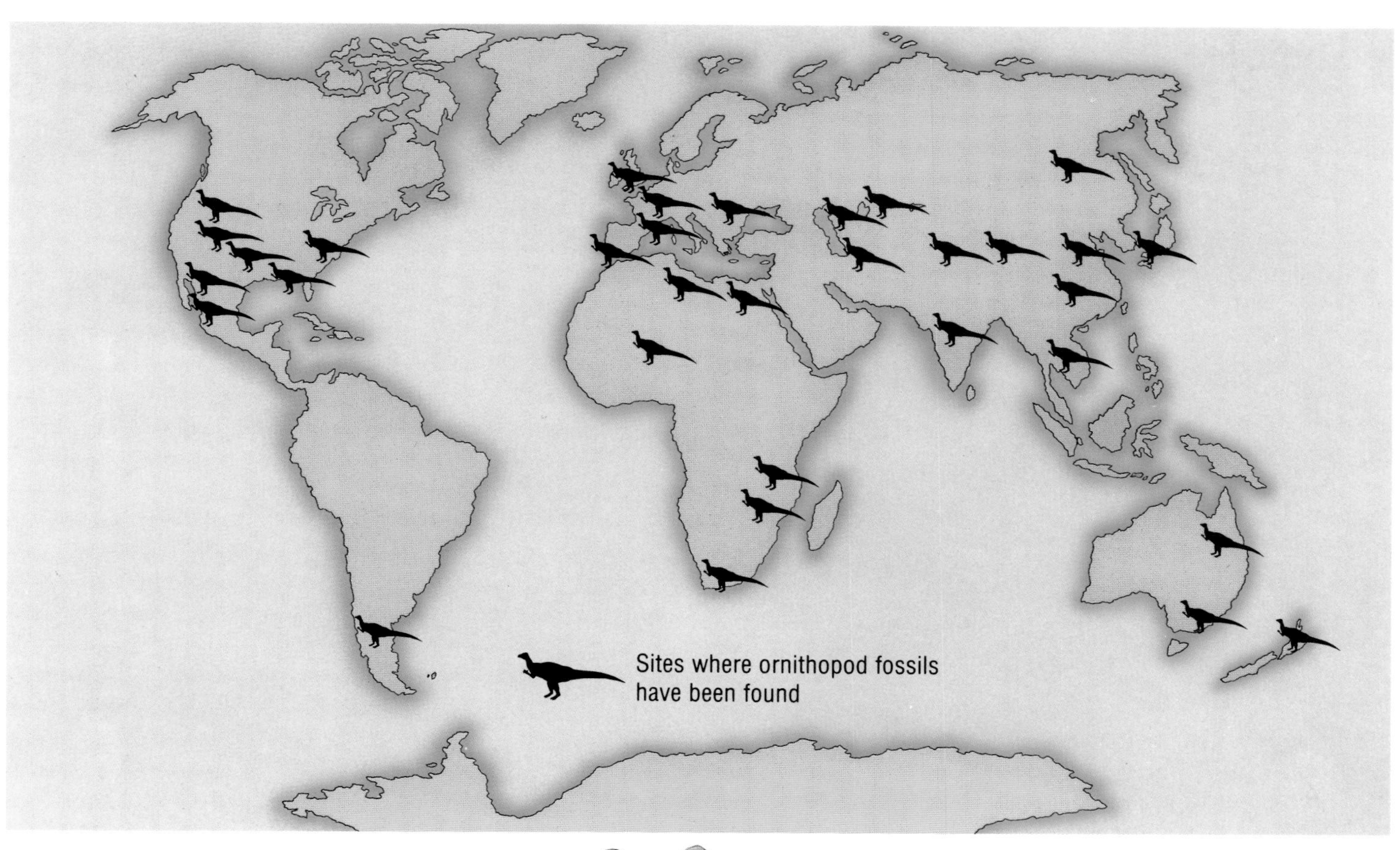

▲ *Fossils of the pre-ornithopods, the fabrosaurids, have been found in South Africa and northern lands. The hypsilophodontids lived worldwide. Camptosaurid and iguanodontid fossils come from Europe and North America. Duckbilled dinosaurs are mostly known from fossils in North America and East Asia.*

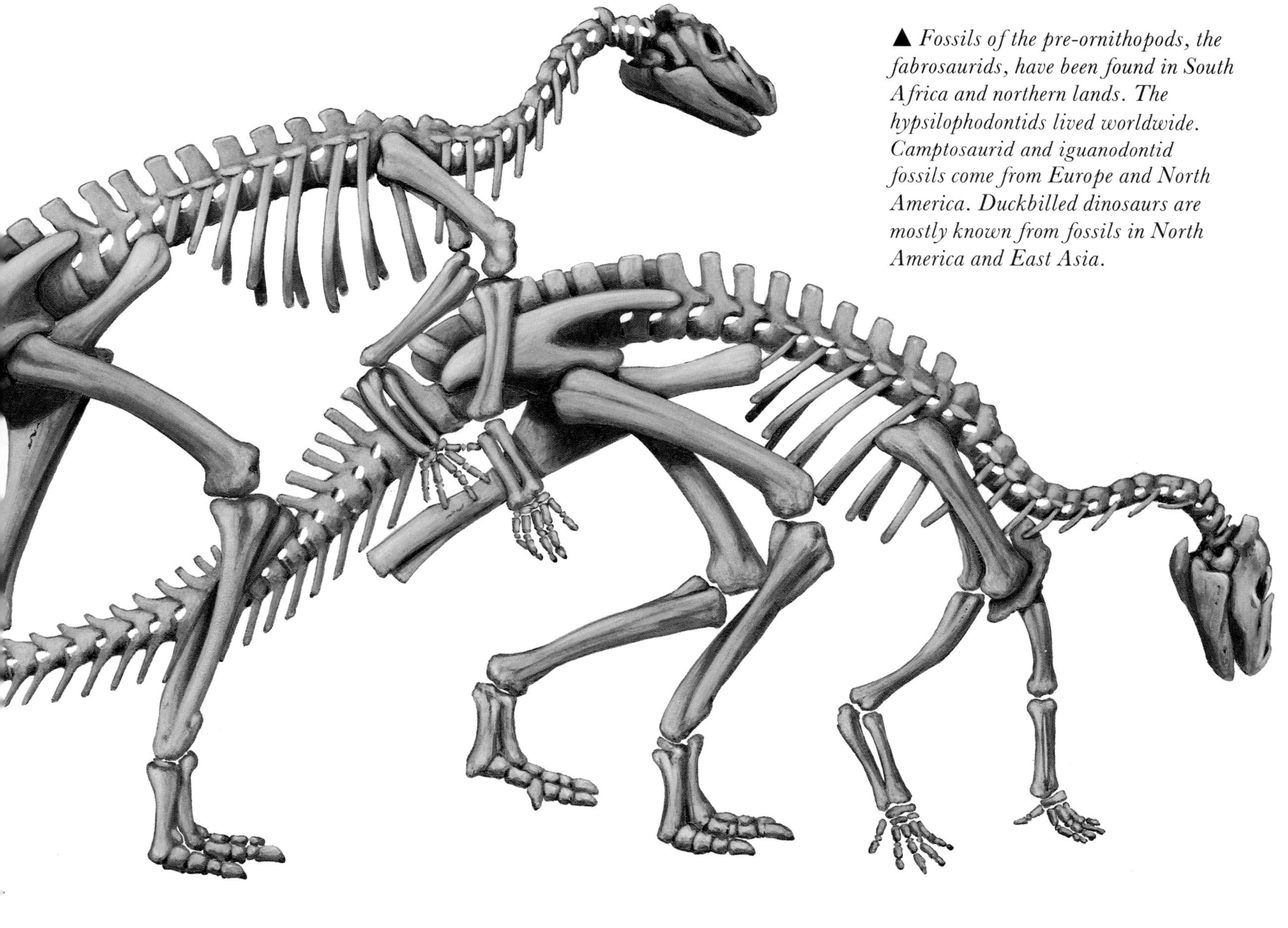

▲ *A* Camptosaurus *rears up on its hind legs to browse in Late Jurassic times. From early ornithopods such as this came dinosaurs such as* Iguanodon *and* Corythosaurus. *Although these two later dinosaurs were bigger than* Camptosaurus, *their bodies were both built in much the same way.*

▼ Iguanodon *was one of the first dinosaurs to be discovered. When scientists first tried to rebuild this large plant-eater they mistook its spiky thumbs for horns.*

One of the best known of these dinosaurs was *Hypsilophodon*. Fossil remains show that *Hypsilophodon* lived in Early Cretaceous times. One of its distinctive features was its big cheek teeth. Chewing tough plants can make teeth go very blunt, but *Hypsilophodon*'s ridged top and bottom cheek teeth sharpened one another as the dinosaur chewed. *Hypsilophodon* only grew up to 6 feet long, but its long shins and elongated four-toed feet meant that it could quickly run away from danger. Big, keen eyes spotted any enemy as it drew near.

A bulky browser

From small, early ornithopods came much bigger animals such as the camptosaurids ("bent reptiles"). Among the largest members of this family was *Camptosaurus*. An adult *Camptosaurus* could grow as big as a large rhinoceros.

Such large creatures needed a lot more food to keep them alive than smaller dinosaurs such as *Hypsilophodon*. *Camptosaurus* developed a broader beak, a longer snout, and larger, more powerful jaws than its smaller ancestors. This allowed it to break off and chew more food with every bite.

Camptosaurus looked a bit like a big, bulky flesh-eater when it stood on its long, strong hind legs. But whereas flesh-eating dinosaurs always walked on their hind limbs, *Camptosaurus* often stood and walked on all fours. We know this from the shape of its thigh bones and claws. The thigh bones of this "bent reptile" were long and curved, not short and straight like those of animals that run fast on their hind limbs. Its claws were like short, blunt hooves, not long, sharp hooks. They were shaped for bearing weight, not for grasping prey. Scientists believe that *Camptosaurus* usually walked on all fours but that it could rear up on its hind legs to reach leafy twigs high up on trees.

"Iguana tooth"

Iguanodontids ("iguana teeth") were medium to big dinosaurs similar to camptosaurids. However, they seem to have had more teeth, straighter thigh bones, and bigger arms than animals such as *Camptosaurus*.

The best known iguanodontid is easily *Iguanodon*. A large, full-grown *Iguanodon* measured up to 30 feet long and could weigh as much as an elephant. If it were alive today, a big *Iguanodon* could have stood on its hind limbs and raised its head as high as a second-story window. Like *Camptosaurus*, however, *Iguanodon* usually walked on all fours, resting the front part of its body on the hoof-shaped nails of the three strong, middle fingers of each hand.

Iguanodon's hands did more than simply help bear the dinosaur's massive weight; they probably helped it to feed and

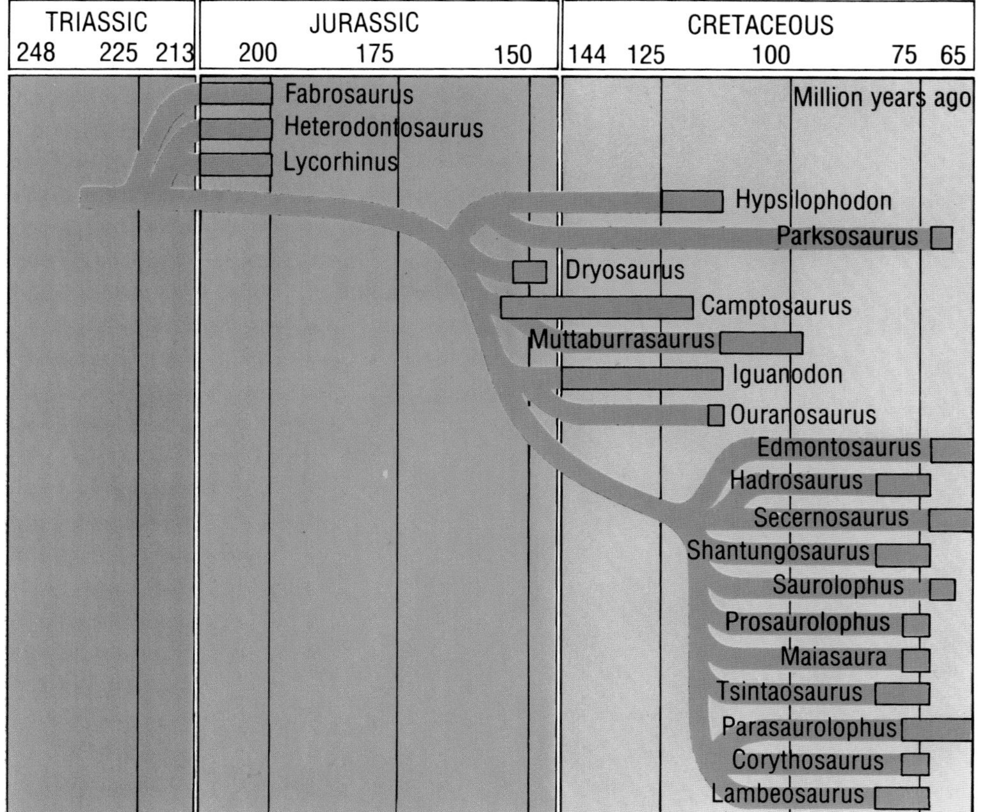

◀ *Early ornithopods such as* Heterodontosaurus *and* Lycorhinus *were to lead to much larger dinosaurs.* Parksosaurus *was one of the last hypsilophodontids, while* Muttaburrasaurus *is one of the few ornithopods to have been uncovered in Australia.* Ouranosaurus *had a sail on its back. The duckbilled dinosaurs lived later than most other ornithopods.*

fend off enemies as well. *Iguanodon*'s little finger was more flexible than the other four and could have been used as a hook to pull leafy twigs down to its mouth. Its thumbs were stiff and spiked. *Iguanodon* may have used these sharp spikes as daggers to defend itself with. They could have blinded an attacking *Megalosaurus*, or at least punched painful gashes in the carnosaur's tough hide.

Iguanodon's life was usually peaceful, however. It probably spent most of the day munching leaves that it had snipped off with its horny beak. A long tongue may have helped to pull these into its mouth, where more than 100 strong, closely packed cheek teeth chewed them up. While an *Iguanodon* browsed, it would have kept a sharp lookout for any hungry enemies. At the least sign of danger it probably hurried off on its long hind limbs with its flattened tail held out stiffly behind to balance it. Even an armed ornithopod would rather run away than risk a fight!

Duckbilled dinosaurs

Many of the dinosaurs that have been uncovered seem strange to us. But perhaps some of the strangest dinosaurs of all were the hadrosaurids, or "big reptiles." These dinosaurs had a broad, toothless beak like a duck's, so many people call them duckbilled dinosaurs.

Hadrosaurids appeared relatively late in the Age of Dinosaurs and included some of the largest of all ornithopods. *Lambeosaurus* ("Lambe's reptile"), from North America, and

ORNITHOPOD FAMILIES

Fossil nests, eggs, and dinosaur young that have been found in the United States tell us much about ornithopod family life. Although it is now thought that some ornithopod young could run about as soon as they hatched, the young of the duckbilled dinosaur *Maiasaura* probably depended on their mother to bring food to their nest. These nests were 6 feet across, 2.5 feet deep, and were lined with leaves. *Maiasaura* mothers built their nests close together for greater protection, much as seabirds do. They may even have returned to the same nests year after year.

▼ Corythosaurus *is one of the best known of the duckbilled dinosaurs. Its semicircular crest may have been used to make loud bellowing noises or honking sounds.*

Shantungosaurus ("Shantung reptile"), from China, were as long as four small cars parked end to end.

Hadrosaurids were built very like their iguanodontid ancestors, except that they had deeper tails and longer limbs. Also, their four-fingered hands were shaped as padded paws. At one time many scientists believed that the hadrosaurids lived in water. Today, however, most people agree that they lived on dry land most of the time, although they may have escaped to the water when attacked.

Hadrosaurids had more teeth than any other dinosaur – up to 2,000 set side by side in rows. When the old teeth wore down, new ones grew up, pushed them out and took their place. As

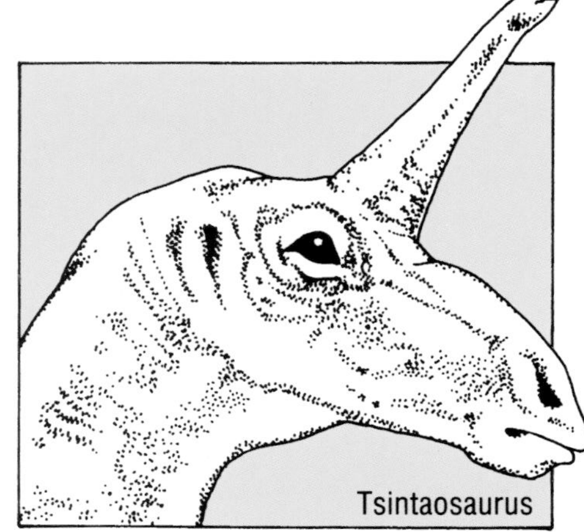

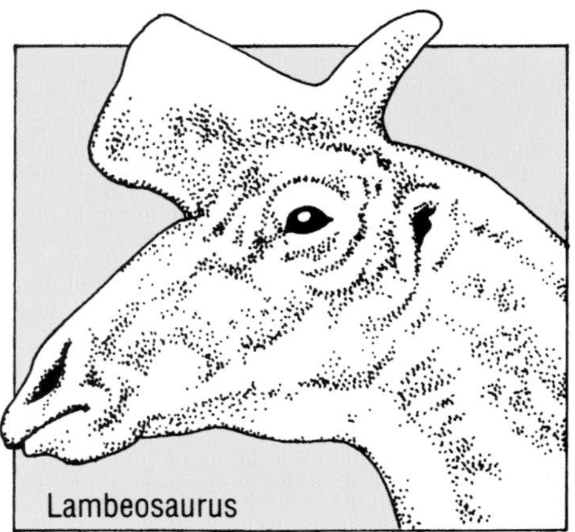

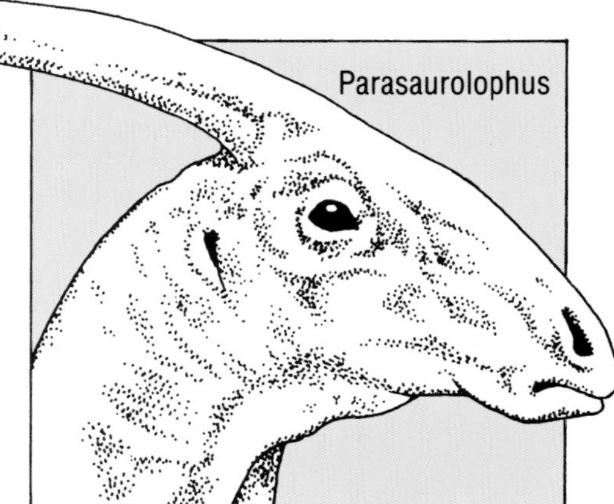

▲ *No duckbilled dinosaurs had stranger heads than these.* Tsintaosaurus *seems to have had a tall, bony spike like a unicorn's horn.* Lambeosaurus *had a bony crest shaped like a hatchet with a spike at the back, while* Parasaurolophus *had a bony tube 5 feet long that jutted back from its head.*

► *Two* Edmontosaurus *and a* Parasaurolophus *browse on conifers and other vegetation while keeping a sharp lookout for any sign of danger.*

hadrosaurids chewed, their top and bottom teeth sharpened one another. This helped them to mash up their tough plant food. We know what they ate because fossil twigs and leaves have been found inside the remains of one fossil hadrosaurid.

▲ *This hatching duckbill was quite small and defenseless. Its parents would have fed it and cared for it until it was old enough to look after itself.*

Crests and hooters

What made the duckbilled dinosaurs such curious creatures was the shape of their heads. Different kinds of duckbill evolved strange crests and horns. *Edmontosaurus*, for example, had a low, flat skull that was possibly covered with loose skin. *Saurolopus* ("ridged reptile") is also thought to have had loose skin flaps on its face, but, in addition, it had a solid, bony spike that jutted back over its neck. *Corythosaurus* ("helmeted reptile") had a tall, narrow, semi-circular crest stuck on its head, while *Parasaurolophus* had a long, hollow tube that swept back over its neck – perhaps a built-in hooter. Females and young had smaller crests than males so people once mistook them for "new" species.

Nobody knows for certain what these crests and hooters were for. Maybe the different crests helped each duckbill recognize others of its own kind. It is also possible that duckbills such as *Edmontosaurus* inflated the loose flaps of skin on their faces to make loud, bellowing calls. These could have been used to attract or warn other dinosaurs in their group.

armored animals

▼ Stegosaurus *roamed through glades and woods like this in Late Jurassic North America. The plated dinosaurs shared their world with the feathered* Archaeopteryx, *whose cries may have warned the dinosaur of danger. Despite their bony plates and spikes, these big plant-eaters had to stay on guard against attacks from large flesh-eaters such as* Allosaurus.

Several goups of plant-eating dinosaurs developed weapons or wore built-in suits of armor to protect themselves from attacks by hungry carnosaurs. These dinosaurs needed strong defenses as many were heavy beasts that could not run fast enough to escape a big, fierce theropod. Instead, they stood their ground, protected by their bony armor, plates, or horns.

Early ancestors

These armored animals were all bird-hipped dinosaurs with horny beaks. They were descended from small, light, speedy ancestors that ran on long hind limbs. One of these was *Scutellosaurus* ("small-shield reptile"). *Scutellosaurus* was no longer than a young child and had fairly long arms, a long tail, and rows of bony studs down its back. Another early ancestor, *Scelidosaurus* ("limb reptile"), was a bigger, heavier, four-legged creature. Any attacking flesh-eater risked snapping off its teeth on rows of bony plates set in *Scelidosaurus*'s skin like stepping stones.

Plated dinosaurs

From lightly armored ancestors such as *Scelidosaurus* came larger beasts with thicker, stronger armor. Among them were the plated dinosaurs. The biggest and best known of these was *Stegosaurus*.

Stegosaurus grew up to twice as long as *Scelidosaurus* and at the hips stood as high as a room. It may have reared higher still on its hind limbs to browse on leafy branches with its rather feeble-looking teeth. Long, strong thighs and broad feet with hooflike toes helped bear this dinosaur's weight.

Scelidosaurus

▲ *Dinosaurs such as* Scelidosaurus *were the ancestors of all armored and plated dinosaurs.* Scelidosaurus *had only rows of bony bumps to guard its skin. From studs such as these came the long, sharp spikes of* Kentrosaurus, *a stegosaur.*

▼ Ankylosaurus *(bottom) was the largest ankylosaur. In addition to its spiked armor it had a club as big as a man's head on the end of its tail. This mass of bone (below) grew from the dinosaur's tail bones.* Ankylosaurus *would have used it to thump and bruise an attacking flesh-eater.*

Stegosaurus was as heavy as several big horses, yet its tiny head held a brain no bigger than a dog's. A bony hole in the spine above the hips was once thought to hold a second brain, but scientists now believe that this hole was really a meeting place for the nerves that controlled the back legs and tail. It may also have stored a supply of fat for energy.

What made *Stegosaurus* really special, however, was its armor. Triangular bony plates up to 3 feet high ran down its back. Scientists are not sure exactly how these plates were arranged. They may have formed two rows or just one row. They may have stood straight up to guard the spine or flopped out sideways to protect the animal's sides. They may not have been weapons at all, but radiators. If so, on hot days they would have allowed heat to escape to stop *Stegosaurus* from overheating. On chilly mornings, they could have trapped the sun's rays to warm the animal.

As well as bony plates, *Stegosaurus* also sported spikes. Two pairs of spikes stuck out sideways from its tail and could have been used to swipe any carnosaur that crept up from behind. It is also likely that a pair of bony spikes in horny sheaths protected *Stegosaurus'* shoulders.

Armored dinosaurs

Plated dinosaurs of different kinds roamed Jurassic North America, Europe, Africa, and Asia, but most of them had died out by Late Cretaceous times. By then their place had been taken by the best protected of all plant-eating dinosaurs: the armored dinosaurs.

Scientists call these heavy-bodied dinosaurs ankylosaurs, which means "fused reptiles." Bands of horn-covered, bony plates of different sizes stiffened the tough skin that covered

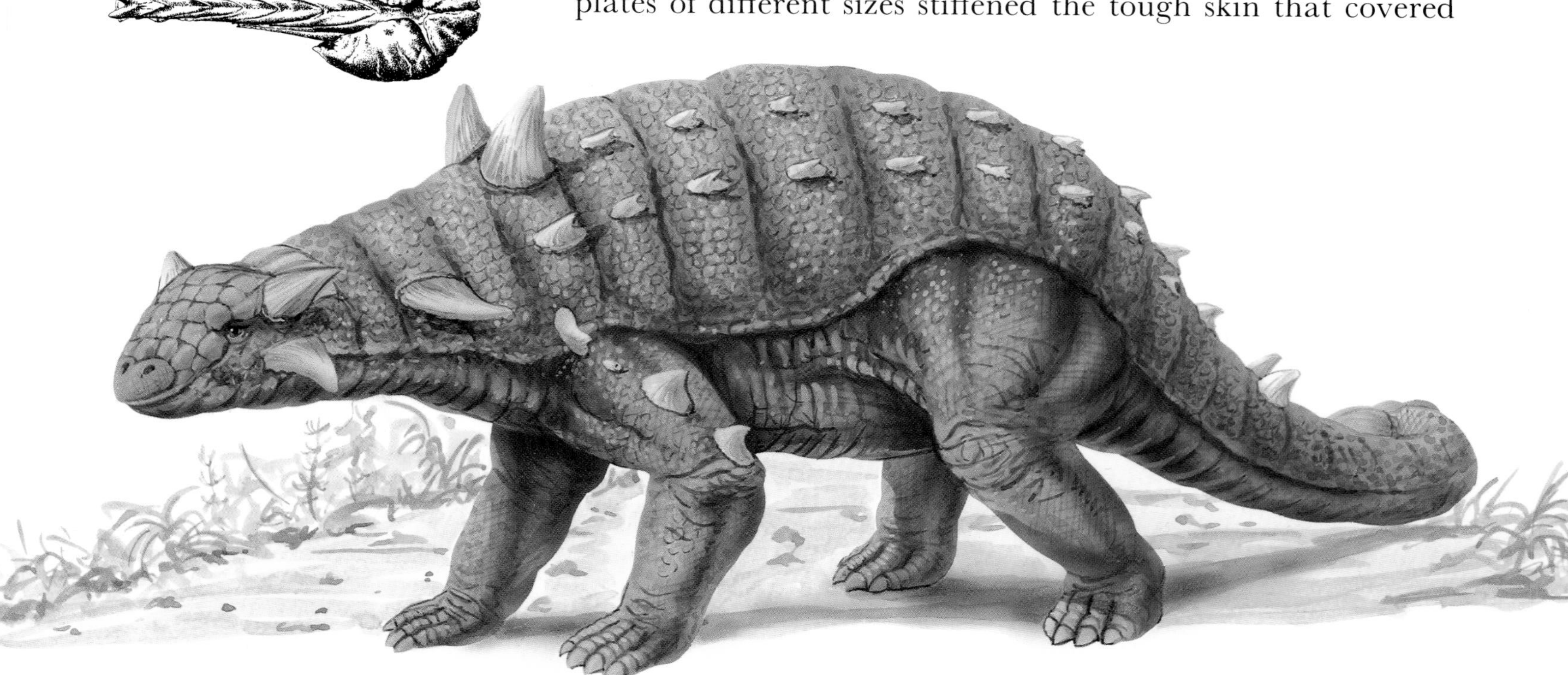

◀ *The fossil skin of the ankylosaur* Euoplocephalus *(left) gives us a good idea of why this dinosaur would have been so hard to attack. Its back was covered with a thick, tough armor made of bony plates and low spikes sheathed with horn. The belly would have been less well protected, but* Euoplocephalus *probably crouched down if attacked. The nodosaurid* Hylaeosaurus *(above) was similarly well protected with spines that stuck out sideways and upwards along its spine and tail.*

the head, neck, back, and sides of these animals. This living suit of armor must have been very heavy to carry around, but it provided excellent protection against an attack by a hungry *Tyrannosaurus*.

An ankylosaur's only weak spot was its soft belly. Scientists have found fossils of ankylosaurs lying on their backs; this may be because they fell into a river and drowned, but it is also possible that some carnosaurs were clever enough to roll an ankylosaur upside down to attack it.

Early ankylosaurs

The first known ankylosaur, *Sarcolestes* ("flesh-robber"), lived in what is now England about 170 million years ago. By Early Cretaceous times, this region was home to other ankylosaurs. One of them was *Hylaeosaurus*. *Hylaeosaurus* was as long as a car; it had a small head, powerful limbs, and a heavy tail. Rows of armored plates protected the top of its neck and back, while a bony corset with small bumps shielded the hips. Two rows of bony plates guarded the tail, and spikes probably stuck out from the sides and legs.

Two groups of ankylosaurs

The ankylosaurs can be divided into two families: the nodosaurids, or "node reptiles," and the ankylosaurids. *Sarcolestes* and *Hylaeosaurus* were both nodosaurids. Nodosaurids had a fairly narrow head and a pointed snout. Some had spines jutting from their sides. They fed on low-growing plants, which they cropped with their horny beaks. Inside their massive

ARMORED ANIMAL RECORDS
(length in feet)

Largest Armored Animals	
Stegosaurs	
Stegosaurus:	30
Ankylosaurs	
Ankylosaurus:	35
Pachycephalosaurs	
Pachycephalosaurus:	15
Ceratopsians	
Triceratops:	30
Smallest Armored Animals	
Stegosaurs	
Dravidosaurus:	10
Ankylosaurs	
Struthiosaurus:	6
Pachycephalosaurs	
Wannanosaurus:	2
Ceratopsians	
Bagaceratops:	3

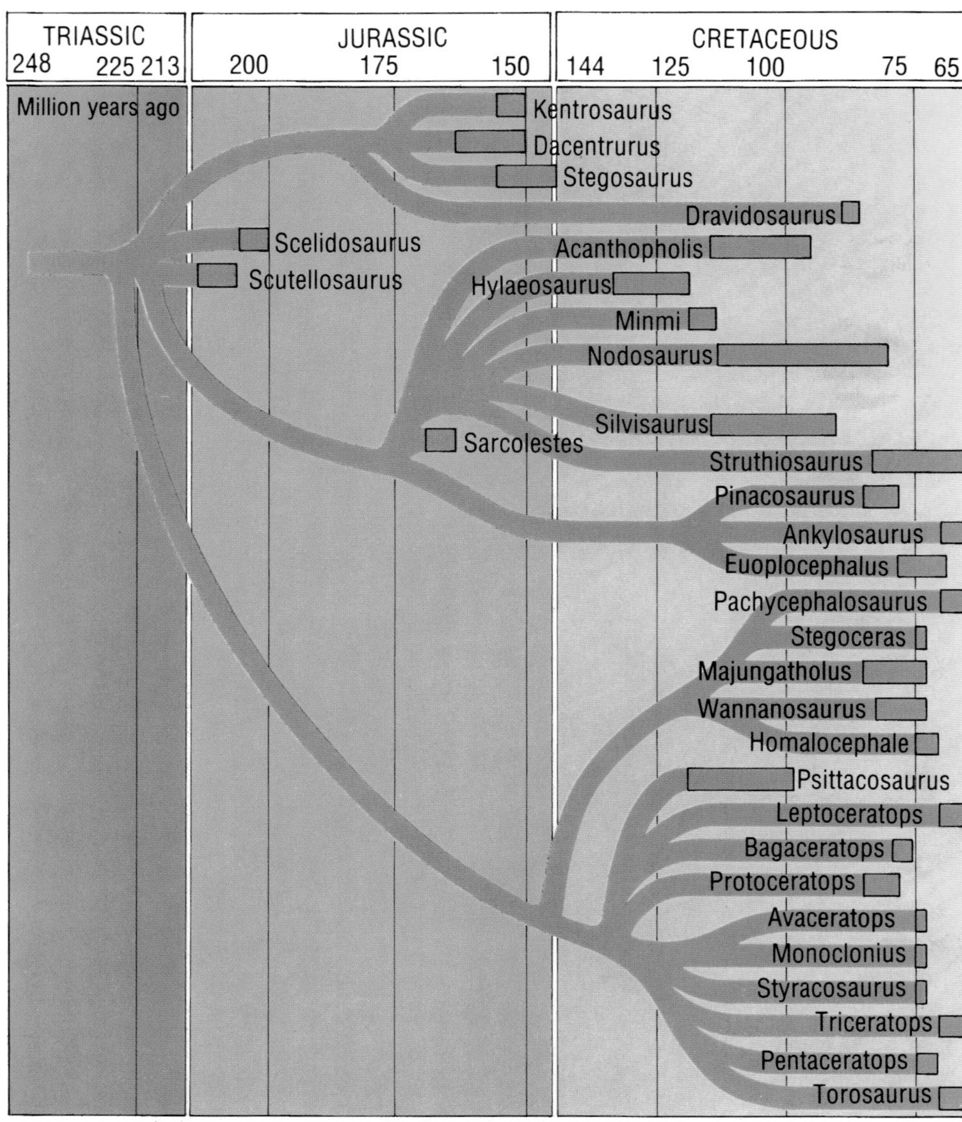

◀ *This family tree shows how the different groups of armored animals were related.* Dacentrurus *was one of the earliest stegosaurids.* Acanthopholis *and* Minmi *were both nodosaurids.* Minmi *is the only known Australian ankylosaur. The ankylosaurid* Pinacosaurus *had a pointed parrotlike beak. The domed pachycephalosaur* Majungatholus, *is known only from its skull, unlike the flat-headed* Homalocephale, *which is known from an almost complete skeleton. From early protoceratopsids such as* Bagaceratops *came larger creatures such as* Monoclonius.

jaws were rows of tiny, leaf-shaped teeth. Nodosaurids walked with their bodies held high off the ground, but they probably crouched down when attacked to protect their bellies.

Ankylosaurids were much like nodosaurids. Both groups had short necks, heavy bodies, strong limbs, and long tails. But an ankylosaurid's head was much wider and it had no long spines jutting out from its sides. Instead, its long tail ended in a bony club. On the whole, ankylosaurids were larger than most nodosaurids, and at 35 feet long, *Ankylosaurus* may have been the largest of all the armored dinosaurs.

Bone-headed battering rams

Bone-headed dinosaurs were among the strangest of all plant-eating dinosaurs. Like small ornithopods, they had short arms and walked on their long hind limbs. But because of their thick skull roofs, scientists class them in a separate group called the pachycephalosaurs, or "thick-headed reptiles."

There were probably two groups of boneheads by Late Cretaceous times. One had thick, flat skulls, while the other had skulls that were high and rounded, like a dome. The two best

▼ *Rival stags lock antlers to decide who should rule the herd. Stags are mammals, but they fight much as the boneheads must have done.*

▼ *Skull met skull with a loud bang when two boneheads fought. Males bashed their heads together to decide who should be master of a bonehead herd. This punishment would crack open any ordinary skull. But the skull of* Pachycephalosaurus *was so thick that there was no damage to the bone or to the brain inside.*

LIVING BATTERING RAMS

The body of the pachycephalosaur *Stegoceras* was built to withstand the force of a head butting fight with a rival dinosaur. *Stegoceras*'s high-domed skull was very thick, and solid bones round the back of its skull gave added protection. The animal's backbone and hip bones were also especially strong so as to absorb the impact of the collision. Fossil skulls of young dinosaurs are thinner than adult skulls and show that *Stegoceras*'s skull got thicker as it grew older. Adult skulls of different thicknesses have also been found. These suggest that female skulls were not as thick as those of males.

known kinds of domed bonehead were *Stegoceras* ("horny roof") and *Pachycephalosaurus* ("thick-headed reptile"). *Stegoceras* had a skull roof that was five times thicker than a human's, with a low, bony fringe around the back of the skull. Yet this dinosaur stood no taller than a man and its brain was as small as a hen's egg. *Pachycephalosaurus* was bigger and even more unusual. Its skull was five times thicker than that of *Stegoceras*. Bony spikes stuck up from the snout and sharp knobs rose up from around the back of the skull.

For a long time scientists wondered why these harmless plant-eaters needed armored heads; they would have been no defense against a hungry carnosaur. Eventually scientists realized that bonehead males must have used their heads for fighting duels. The male flatheads would have pushed against each other with their heads. The male domeheads would have run at one another and banged their heads together hard. Rival mountain sheep, stags, and sea lizards still fight in both these ways today.

"Parrot reptiles"

Far more plentiful than the pachycephalosaurs or ankylosaurs were the horned dinosaurs. Scientists have found enough skull and skeletons of these rhinoceros-like creatures to tell us how they evolved and how they lived.

We can be fairly sure that horned dinosaurs evolved from animals such as *Psittacosaurus*. This two-legged creature grew 6 feet long and walked and ran (not very fast) on long hind limbs, balanced by its tail. Sometimes it may have walked on

► *A* Psittacosaurus *crops leaves with its deep, sharp beak. People once thought that this dinosaur was a bird-hipped biped, but its parrotlike beak shows it was really an ancestor of the horned dinosaurs.* Psittacosaurus*'s short arms could have been used to bring leafy branches to its mouth, although its blunt hooves suggest that it may sometimes have walked on all fours. Most* Psittacosaurus *fossils have been found in Mongolia, China, and Siberia.*

◀ *Two adult* Protoceratops *keep watch for enemies as three of their young crouch low on the sandy ground. Fossil finds have shown scientists that these babies hatched from eggs laid in a hollow in the sand. Their mother probably guarded her buried eggs until the babies broke out of the shells, just as mother crocodiles and pythons take care of their eggs today.*

all fours, using its "hands." These ended in blunt claws and could also have pulled leaves down to *Psittacosaurus*'s deep, narrow beak. Like a parrot's beak, this was ideally shaped for chopping up tough leaves from the flowering plants that were just becoming plentiful.

A parrotlike beak was a feature shared by *Psittacosaurus* and all its horned relatives. Indeed, scientists class all these dinosaurs together as ceratopsians, or "horned faces." Early ceratopsians had no horns, just spiky cheeks, and they were small and defenseless compared with the big horned dinosaurs that evolved later: In between, however, came the protoceratopsids, or "first horned faces."

"First horned faces"

The protoceratopsids had features common to both the psittacosaurids and the big horned dinosaurs. They were smaller than the big horned dinosaurs and had bony bumps instead of long horns on their heads. Some still had clawed toes and fingers like *Psittacosaurus*, instead of the hooflike nails of later ceratopsids. Little *Leptoceratops* ("slim horned face") could probably still run on its hind limbs. Heavier beasts such as *Protoceratops* walked on all fours and had big heads that were nearly three-fourths the length of their backs. A flat crest that jutted back over the neck and shoulders formed a shield to guard the animals' nerves and blood vessels. This bony frill also anchored the powerful muscles that held up the heavy jaws and head. Strong jaw muscles worked the beak that chopped off the tough leaves on which *Protoceratops* fed. Sharp, shearing cheek teeth then chopped these up into a pulp ready for swallowing.

▼ *This fossil skull of a* Triceratops *shows just how formidable this dinosaur must have been. The long horns jutting out from its forehead measured nearly 3 feet long. Another, smaller, horn grew on its nose. The bony frill that protected the animal's neck was not as long as on some other ceratopsids such as* Torosaurus, *but its back edge was surrounded by a zigzag of bony knobs. Weighing up to 5.4 tons and measuring 30 feet long,* Triceratops *was well able to defend itself against any attacker.*

Dinosaur rhinos

The big horned dinosaurs that appeared later in the Cretaceous were far bigger and better armed than the protoceratopsids. Compare *Protoceratops* with *Triceratops*, for instance. *Protoceratops* grew no longer than a man and only had thickened bone above the snout and eyes *Triceratops* reached 30 feet and weighed more than a bull elephant. Instead of bony bumps, its head bore three sharp horns.

With its horned head, bulky body, and strong, thick legs *Triceratops* looked rather like a giant rhinoceros. But the great head had a short, bony neck frill, a deep, narrow beak like a parrot's, and row on row of sharp, shearing cheek teeth. The horn above its nose was short, but two horns about 3 feet long stuck out above its eyes.

Triceratops was the largest of the horned dinosaurs, but there were others just as strange. *Styracosaurus* had six long spikes sticking out from around its frill. *Torosaurus* ("bull reptile")

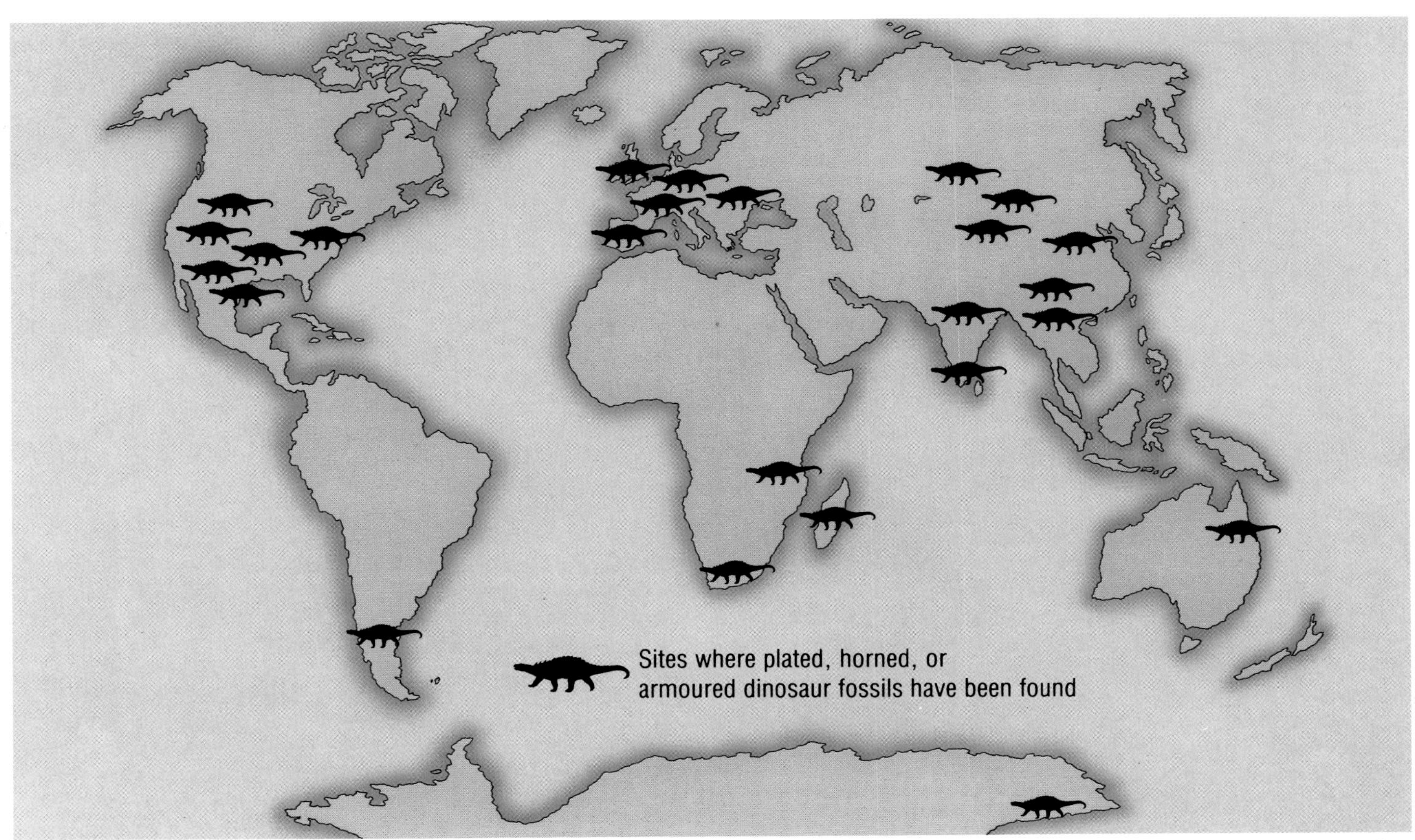

had the largest head of any land animal, while *Pentaceratops* had an immense neck frill, and cheeks with large, hornlike knobs.

It is very likely that these horned monsters lived in herds. If a big flesh-eater came too close, they probably formed a protective ring around their young while the big males charged the enemy to drive it away. Male ceratopsids may also have used their horns to fight duels.

▲ *Stegosaur bones have been found in Africa, Asia, Europe, and North America. Ankylosaur fossils come from Asia, Antarctica, Australia, Europe, and North America. Protoceratopsids are known from Asia and South America, but the big horned dinosaurs lived in what is now North America.*

◀ *A* Triceratops *plunges its horns into a startled* Tyrannosaurus. *The big horned dinosaur was capable of punching deep holes into the scared carnosaur. Carnosaurs probably dared not attack a healthy, fully grown* Triceratops.

DINOSAUR HERDS

Fossils of horned dinosaurs are more plentiful than those of almost any other dinosaur. In parts of North America, scientists have found over 100 skeletons of one kind of horned dinosaur all packed together in the rocks. Experts believe that these dinosaurs once belonged to a huge migrating herd that had to swim across a river as it wandered around in search of food. Many of the dinosaurs could have drowned in the crossing and their bodies would then have been washed up on a mudbank. Mass drownings like this still kill hundreds of wildebeeste on the plains of Africa.

fliers and divers

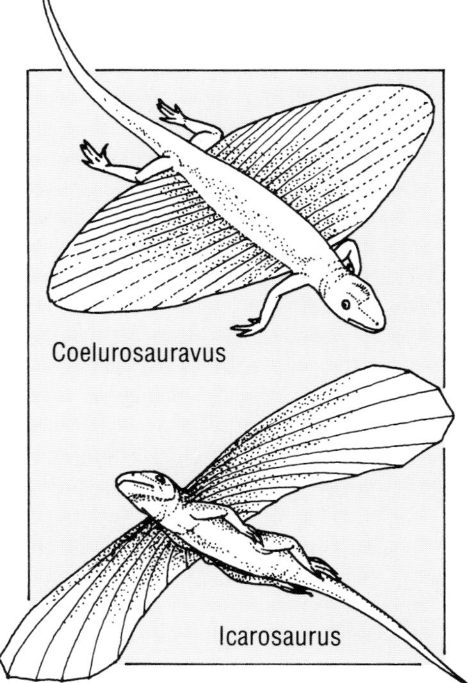

▲ Coelurosauravus *and* Icarosaurus *were early reptile gliders. These reptiles could not fly, but they jumped off trees and glided down on skin wings that were stretched over long ribs.*

While dinosaurs ruled the land, other backboned creatures became masters of the air and waters.

Animals that could fly had big advantages. They could swoop down on fish or snap up flying insects that were out of reach of the dinosaurs. A flying animal could zoom off into the air to escape a hungry predator and could also nest in safety, high up on cliffs or in trees.

Fliers and gliders were specially designed for flight, with wings and lightweight bodies. They also had keen eyes to help them spot food on the ground below, a good sense of balance and the ability to steer in the wind. Two great groups of flying animals arose: the birds and the pterosaurs ("winged reptiles"). Pterosaurs came first.

"Winged reptiles"

Pterosaurs came in many sizes. Some were as small as a sparrow, others as large as a small plane. Their skeletons were made up of long, light, hollow bones. These tubes probably held air to make them lighter, just as birds' bones do. The front edges of their wings of skin were attached to immensely long fourth-finger bones. The back edges joined the body just in front of the legs.

Many pterosaurs had muscles that were strong enough to flap their wings, but others were probably too big and heavy to take off under their own power. These hitched a lift on moving air instead, gliding on currents of warm air on long, narrow wings that were especially good for this kind of flight.

Pterosaurs seem to have been less at home on land than in the air. Many scientists believe that all pterosaurs shuffled awkwardly along on all fours. One scientist, however, thought that at least some kinds of pterosaur could walk and run on their hind limbs. It is possible that they clawed their way up trees with the three fingers on each wing. There, they may have hung upside down to sleep, like bats.

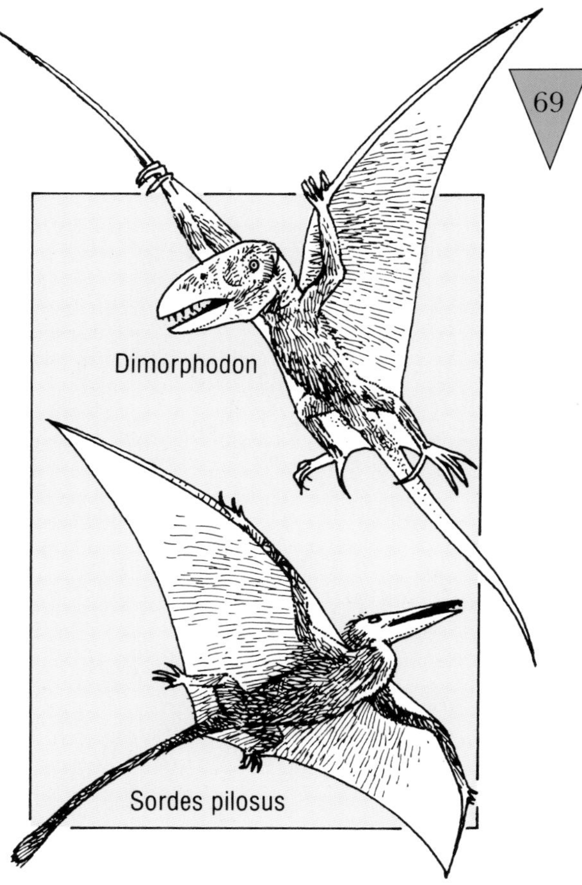

▲ Dimorphodon *had a big, toothy head and a long tail.* Sordes pilosus *had a furry body. Both were Jurassic pterosaurs.*

How pterosaurs began

Pterosaurs appeared mysteriously in Late Triassic times. Some scientists suspect that they came from climbing reptiles, but the closest relatives we know of were the same running reptiles that gave rise to the dinosaurs. Scientists have dug up about 100 species altogether. All come from two main groups.

"Prow beaks"

The first pterosaurs were **rhamphorhynchoids**, or "prow beaks." Most had fairly short faces with beaklike jaws that brimmed with sharp teeth. They had short necks, but their tails were long and acted as a rudder. Fossils have been found that show that most rhamphorhynchoids had fur-covered bodies. One of these was *Sordes pilosus* ("hairy devil"). Fur would have helped to keep its body warm, so that it could store extra energy for flying.

"Prow beaks" had died out by Late Jurassic times. But their place was taken by new flying animals: the birds and those other pterosaurs, the **pterodactyloids** ("winged fingers").

◀ *Slim jaws, sharp teeth, skin wings, and a long, bony tail show up clearly in this* Rhamphorhynchus *fossil. This long-tailed kind of pterosaur probably caught fish. The tail helped to keep its body balanced in the air.*

▶ *A* Pteranodon *parent feeds its young on a sea cliff ledge. The* Pteranodon *would have swooped down to pluck fish from the sea, then soared back up on the wind blowing up the cliffs. Now it hangs in the air and spits out the fish for its young.*

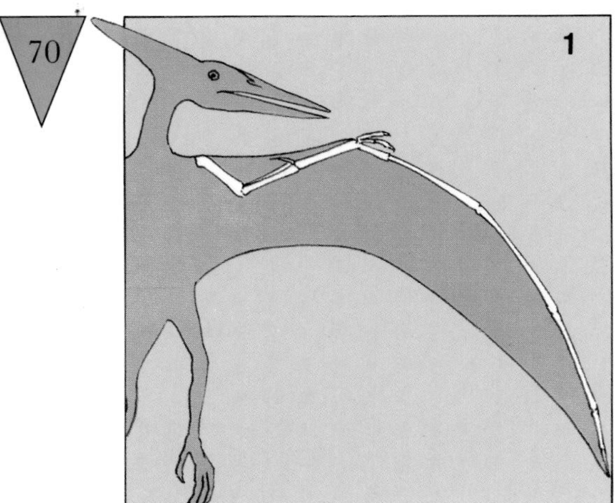

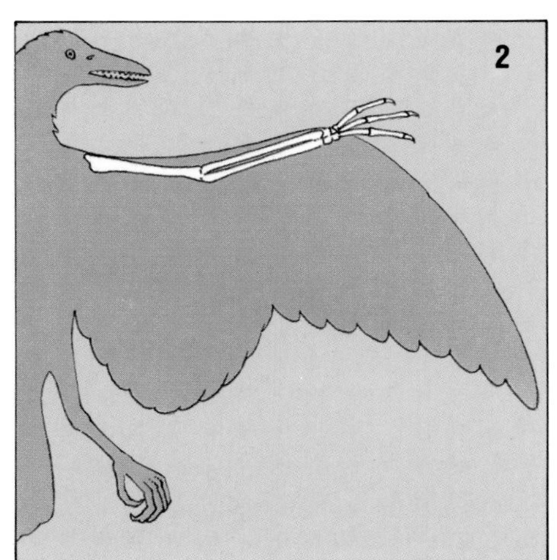

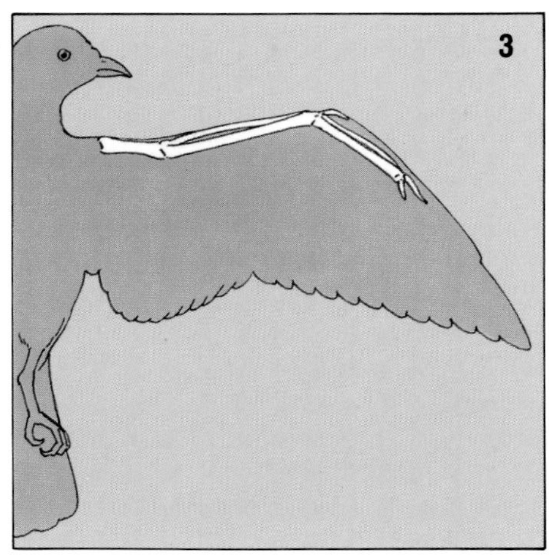

▲ *The wings of a pterosaur (1), an early bird (2), and a modern bird (3). A pterosaur's wings were webs of skin stretched between its body and its immensely long fourth-finger bones.* Archaeopteryx *had feathers, but it still had clawed hands and a toothy beak. Modern birds have feathered wings supported by arm, wrist, and finger bones.*

"Winged fingers"

Pterodactyloids flourished from Late Jurassic to Late Cretaceous times. These pterosaurs tended to have shorter tails than the "prow beaks," but longer necks and heads. Strange pterodactyloids included *Dsungaripterus* ("wing from Jungarr") with its spiky teeth for spearing fish, and *Pterodaustro* ("southern wing") with its hundreds of long, slim teeth that formed a sieve for sifting particles of food from water.

"Winged fingers" tended to increase in size and by Late Cretaceous times some pterodactyloids were huge. *Pteranodon* ("winged and toothless") had only a turkey-sized body, but its wingspan measured up to 23 feet. Even this monster was a midget compared to *Quetzalcoatlus* ("feathered serpent"). With twice *Pteranodon*'s wingspan, this was the largest ever flying creature. In spite of its huge size, *Quetzalcoatlus* somehow soared on updraughts of warm air to scan the plains below for food. It probably zoomed down to feed on dead dinosaurs, as vultures today feed on carrion.

◀ *This splendid fossil* Archaeopteryx *clearly shows not only the bones but the feathers that sprouted from the animal's wings and bony tail. Fossil feathers survive only in very fine-grained rocks. This slab came from a limestone quarry in southern Germany.*

▼ *In real life* Archaeopteryx *may have looked like this. Except for its small, sharp teeth and the bony fingers halfway down its wings, it looked rather like certain birds alive today.*

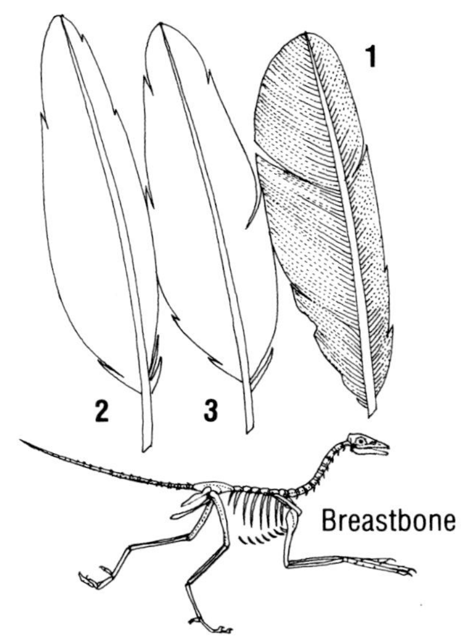

▲ *The feathers of* Archaeopteryx *(1) resemble those of modern birds that fly (2) rather than those of birds that cannot fly (3). But some experts argue that* Archaeopteryx*'s breastbone was too small and weak for flight.*

▼ *The skeleton of a modern bird shows how much stronger its breastbone is when compared to that of* Archaeopteryx.

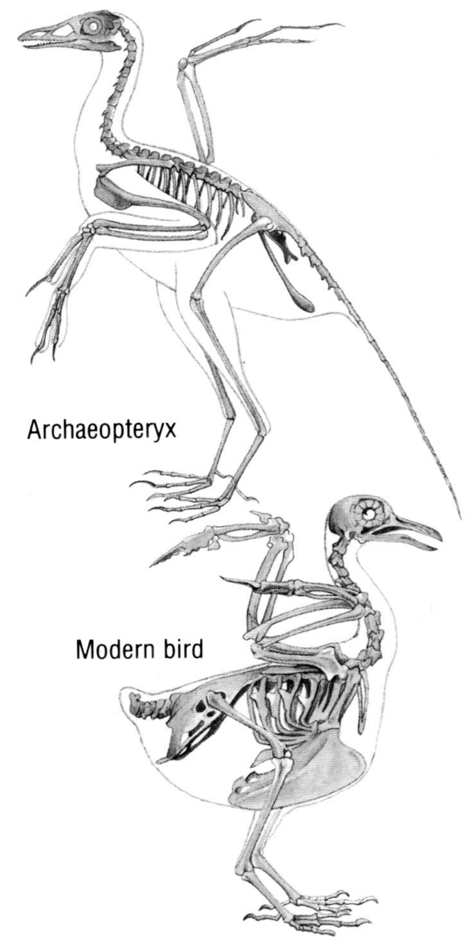

Early birds

Pterosaurs were not the only fliers and gliders. They shared the prehistoric skies with the early ancestors of the birds.

The first known bird was crow-sized *Archaeopteryx* ("ancient wing"). This strange creature probably evolved from small theropods in Late Jurassic times. Like modern birds, *Archaeopteryx* had feathered wings, but, unlike them, its beak bore small, sharp teeth. Clawed fingers stuck out from its wings and it had a long, bony tail. *Archaeopteryx* was probably a feeble flier. It may have run and flapped its wings to take off, but scientists think it is more likely that it clawed its way up trees, then glided or fluttered down.

Early birds like *Archaeopteryx* gave rise to other toothy kinds that resembled modern terns and divers. Later, more modern kinds with toothless beaks appeared. Their feathered wings were better adapted for flight and, as they multiplied, the pterosaurs began to die out. At the end of the Age of Dinosaurs, when dinosaurs and pterosaurs became extinct, the birds survived. Some people believe that the birds are the sole surviving descendants of the dinosaurs.

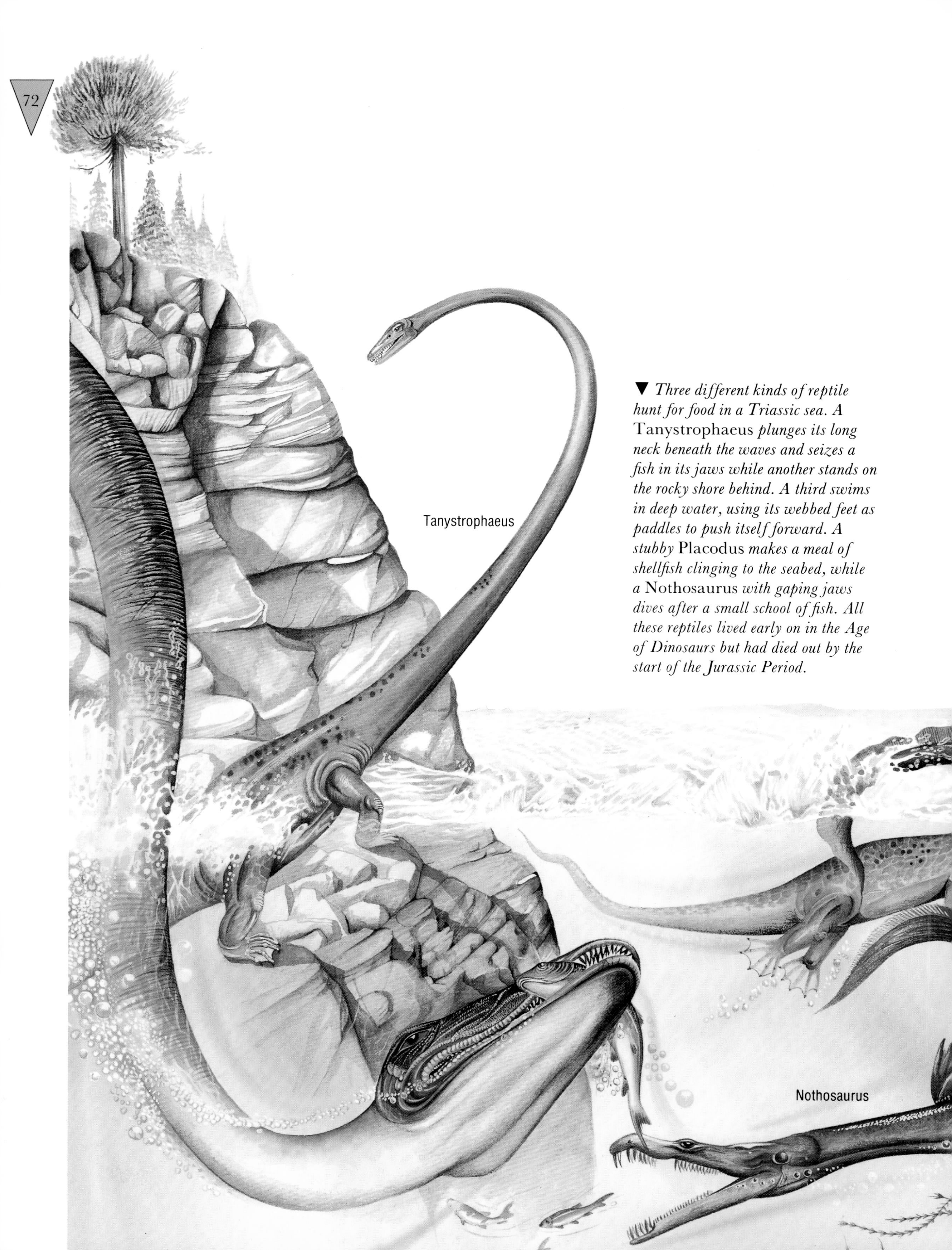

▼ *Three different kinds of reptile hunt for food in a Triassic sea. A* Tanystrophaeus *plunges its long neck beneath the waves and seizes a fish in its jaws while another stands on the rocky shore behind. A third swims in deep water, using its webbed feet as paddles to push itself forward. A stubby* Placodus *makes a meal of shellfish clinging to the seabed, while a* Nothosaurus *with gaping jaws dives after a small school of fish. All these reptiles lived early on in the Age of Dinosaurs but had died out by the start of the Jurassic Period.*

Reptiles take the plunge

While some reptiles took to the air, others became expert swimmers. Several groups discovered food and safety in rivers, lakes, or shallow seas. To begin with, these reptiles just paddled at the water's edge. They probably ate dead fish or munched on shellfish growing on the rocks. Their descendants were better built for catching swimming prey. These later reptiles evolved fins or flippers so that they could swim and dive as nimbly as a fish. They still had to come up for air, however. Sometimes one would haul itself ashore to bask in the sun, lay its eggs, or give birth to its babies. Out of water, the creature could only flop along as awkwardly as a seal. Other water reptiles could not even manage that. These fish-shaped creatures were born under water and spent their lives entirely out at sea.

▲ *This coiled shell was once the home of an ammonite, an extinct sea creature related to the squid and octopus. Tooth marks on some ammonite shells show where they were bitten by big sea reptiles. A juicy ammonite would have made a tasty meal for an ichthyosaur or mosasaur that was able to break open the shell.*

A long-necked angler

Early on in the Age of Dinosaurs lived one of the strangest water reptiles of all. *Tanystrophaeus* ("long twisted neck") had a head, body, legs, and tail like a lizard's, with a neck that was longer than all of these put together. This neck looked like a long, thin pipe and was probably as stiff as a fishing rod. It may have been used as a fishing rod. Perhaps *Tanystrophaeus* kept its feet on dry land while its head plunged underwater to seize fish or shellfish in its sharp teeth. Holding up such a long neck for long periods of time would have been hard work, however. So perhaps this creature lived in shallow water, letting its neck float on the surface.

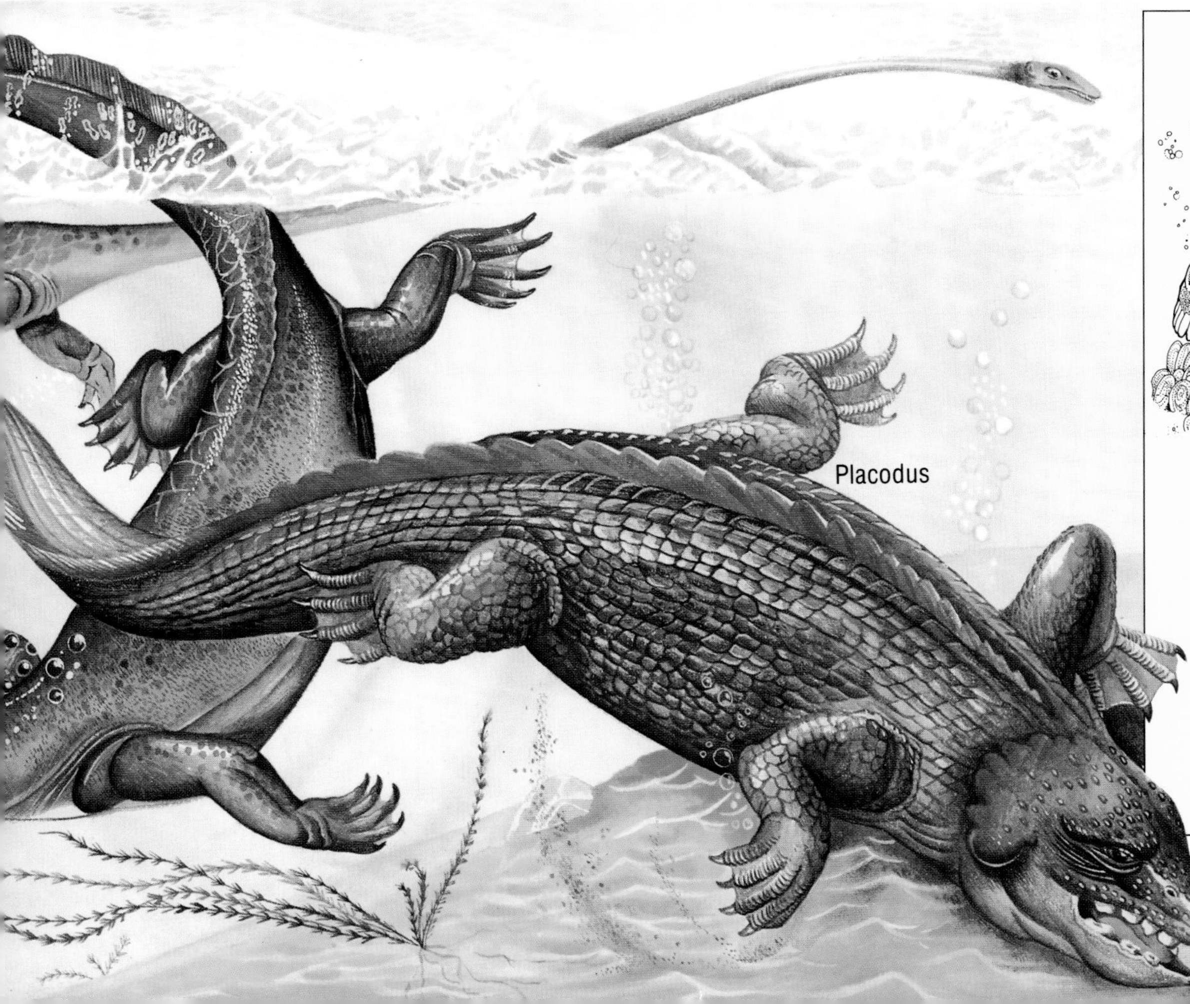

Placodus

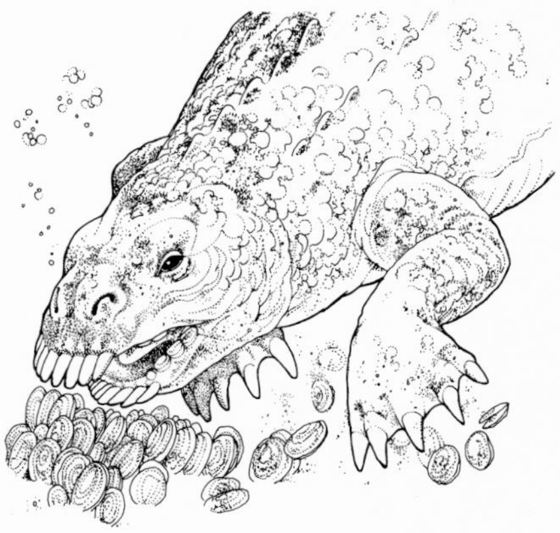

SHELLFISH CRUSHER

A placodont scrapes shellfish off the seabed with its jutting, spoon-shaped front teeth. Powerful jaws then crushed the shells between broad, flat teeth at the back of its mouth so that the reptile could get at the soft animals inside.

▲ *This perfectly preserved fossil ichthyosaur shows the reptile's large eye sockets and long jaws. It is not just the bones that have been preserved, however. The outline of the body of this dolphinlike animal is also clearly visible. Fossil ichthyosaurs come from rocks in lands as far apart as England and Japan.*

SWIMMING METHODS

The reptiles that lived in the sea during the Age of Dinosaurs had evolved bodies that could move easily and efficiently through the water. But different reptiles probably swam in different ways:

Ichthyosaurs
These reptiles were so similar to modern dolphins in shape that it is likely that they also swam in a similar way. By moving their tails and bodies from side to side they would have produced a forward movement. Their fins would have been used to keep their bodies upright in the water.

Turtles
Modern turtles provide clues as to how their prehistoric ancestors swam. Because their bodies were rigid, early turtles would have relied on their flippers to push them through the water.

Plesiosaurs and Pliosaurs
Scientists are still not sure how these marine reptiles swam as they have no modern descendants to compare them with. Perhaps they swam by rowing themselves forward with their flippers. Or maybe they "flew" through the water, moving their flippers in the same way that a bird moves its wing.

"False reptiles"

Nothosaurs ("false reptiles") looked like lizards, but, unlike most lizards, they did not live on land. The smallest nothosaur was no longer than a table knife, but *Nothosaurus* ("false reptile"), one of the largest, grew to the length of a small car. All had long tails, necks, and snouts, and long, sharp teeth for seizing fish. Their legs were strong enough for walking on land, but their feet were possibly webbed for swimming. Early nothosaurs swam by tucking in their short limbs and waggling their bodies and tails. Later nothosaurs had longer, stronger front limbs and did a kind of breast stroke.

Nothosaurs came ashore to breed in caves or on the beach. We know this from discoveries of fossil young. Fossil nothosaurs crop up as far apart as England and Japan. These reptiles must have been extremely plentiful in Mid Triassic times, but by the end of the period they had died out.

Shellfish crunchers

Placodonts ("plate-toothed") looked like nothosaurs with stubby bodies and long tails flattened from side to side. These swimmers hunted shellfish on the seabed. Their front teeth stuck out so that they could seize their prey, which they crunched up between back teeth that were like huge, flat plates. Many placodonts had bits of bone set in their skin to protect them. One peculiar group of placodonts even had a shell a bit like a turtle's and a horny beak instead of teeth at the front of the mouth.

Placodont fossils have been found in rocks from Europe to the Middle East.

"Fish reptiles"

Ichthyosaurs ("fish reptiles") were the fastest swimmers of their age, and perhaps of all time. In short bursts they may have reached speeds of up to 30 miles per hour. With their pointed heads and "neckless," streamlined bodies, these dolphinlike reptiles were superbly built for speed. They swam by arching their bodies back and forth and thrusting water backward with big, upright tailfins. A tall fin jutting up from the back helped to keep them level in the water. To steer and brake, ichthyosaurs used flippers that had evolved from limbs.

◀ *Mosasaurs were lizards that had evolved for life in the sea. Instead of legs, they had developed flippers and a flattened tail that allowed them to move easily through the water. Monitor lizards are their nearest living relatives.*

"Fish reptiles" grew from 10 to 33 feet long. These high-speed hunters searched the seas for fish and for the shellfish known as **ammonites**. Big eyes helped them spot their prey, and sharp teeth seized and crunched their victims. Ichthyosaurs never left the water. They even gave birth to their babies in the sea. Newborn ichthyosaurs at once swam up to the surface to take a breath of air.

Ichthyosaurs appeared before the dinosaurs, but also died out before them, in the early part of the Late Cretaceous. Perhaps they proved no match for the new kinds of shark and other groups of swimming reptiles that had evolved.

▼ *A big pliosaur (a short-necked kind of plesiosaur) seizes a long-necked plesiosaur in its huge, sharp-toothed jaws. Long-necked plesiosaurs probably ate fish and maybe shellfish, but big pliosaurs could kill much larger prey. They were hunters as terrifying as the killer whales roaming the seas today.*

▲ *A giant* Deinosuchus *lunges at an unseen victim; possibly a duckbilled dinosaur similar to the two seen in the distance. This huge crocodile may have preyed mainly on young, small dinosaurs, but it could certainly have drowned a fully grown duckbill.*

▼ *If the two lay side by side,* Deinosuchus *(left) would have dwarfed the biggest modern crocodile (right).* Deinosuchus *grew 50 feet long. Estuarine crocodiles, the largest living crocodiles, are usually less than 16 feet long. Even the longest estuarine crocodile measures less than 30 feet.*

"Meuse reptiles"

Among these new aquatic reptiles were the **mosasaurs**, or "meuse reptiles." These big, snaky reptiles swam in the shallow, offshore waters of Late Cretaceous seas. Limbs like paddles were used for steering as these creatures hunted the ammonites on which they fed. From snout to tail the largest mosasaur measured 30 feet, or more.

"Near reptiles"

The early nothosaurs and placodonts had disappeared by the start of the Jurassic Period. But their descendants, the plesiosaurs ("near reptiles") survived right to the end of the Age of Dinosaurs. These big, flat-bellied monsters were surprisingly good swimmers. They may have swum by pushing water backward with their long front flippers, and steered with stubby tails that served as rudders.

There were two kinds of plesiosaur. One group had small heads and very long necks. This neck took up more than half the length of 40-foot-long *Elasmosaurus* ("thin-plated reptile"). *Elasmosaurus* could have caught fish with quick, stabbing movements of its head.

The short-necked plesiosaurs, or **pliosaurs** ("more reptiles"), had large heads and powerful jaws. Among the largest was the 45-foot-long monster *Kronosaurus* ("Kronos reptile"). *Kronosaurus* would have lain in wait for big fish and other swimming reptiles that swam in the shallow seas that covered much of Late Cretaceous Australia.

Crocodilians

Crocodiles and alligators are the nearest reptile relatives of the dinosaurs still alive today. The first crocodilians were small, short-headed animals that lived on land in Late Triassic times. During the Jurassic Period, large, swimming crocodiles appeared. The strangest of all was seagoing *Geosaurus* ("Earth reptile"), a crocodilian with a broad, flat tail fin, and flippers like a seal's.

The biggest ever crocodile was a 50-foot-long freshwater giant with a head even longer than that of *Tyrannosaurus*. *Deinosuchus* ("fear crocodile") lurked in swamps that covered part of Late Cretaceous North America. Its prey included quite large dinosaurs such as hadrosaurids. Creatures coming down to the river for a drink would mistake *Deinosuchus* for a sunken tree trunk until, suddenly, one end split open to reveal its huge, gaping jaws. By then it was usually too late to escape.

▼ *A loggerhead turtle paddles slowly over a coral reef in the clear, warm waters of the Red Sea. Some modern sea turtles resemble fossils of sea turtles that lived in the Age of Dinosaurs. Instead of a high-domed shell like a tortoise's, sea turtles have low, streamlined shells for speedy swimming. Green turtles can swim faster than most men can run and the leatherback turtle dives as deep as any whale. By looking at the way modern turtles behave, scientists have guessed that turtles in the Age of Dinosaurs could also swim fast and dive deep under the waves.*

Turtles

The ancestors of modern turtles can also be traced back to the Age of Dinosaurs. The first tortoises plodded slowly overland on stumpy legs in Late Triassic times. A heavy, bony "overcoat" protected them from their enemies as they were too heavy and bulky to run away. Eventually, however, these land tortoises gave rise to speedy, lightweight swimmers that lived in fresh water or in the shallow seas of Late Cretaceous North America. Sea turtles developed a much lighter shell and powerful flippers that worked back and forth like a penguin's wings to propel them through the water. *Archelon* ("ruler tortoise") reached a length of 11 feet, which is 3 feet longer than the largest turtle alive today.

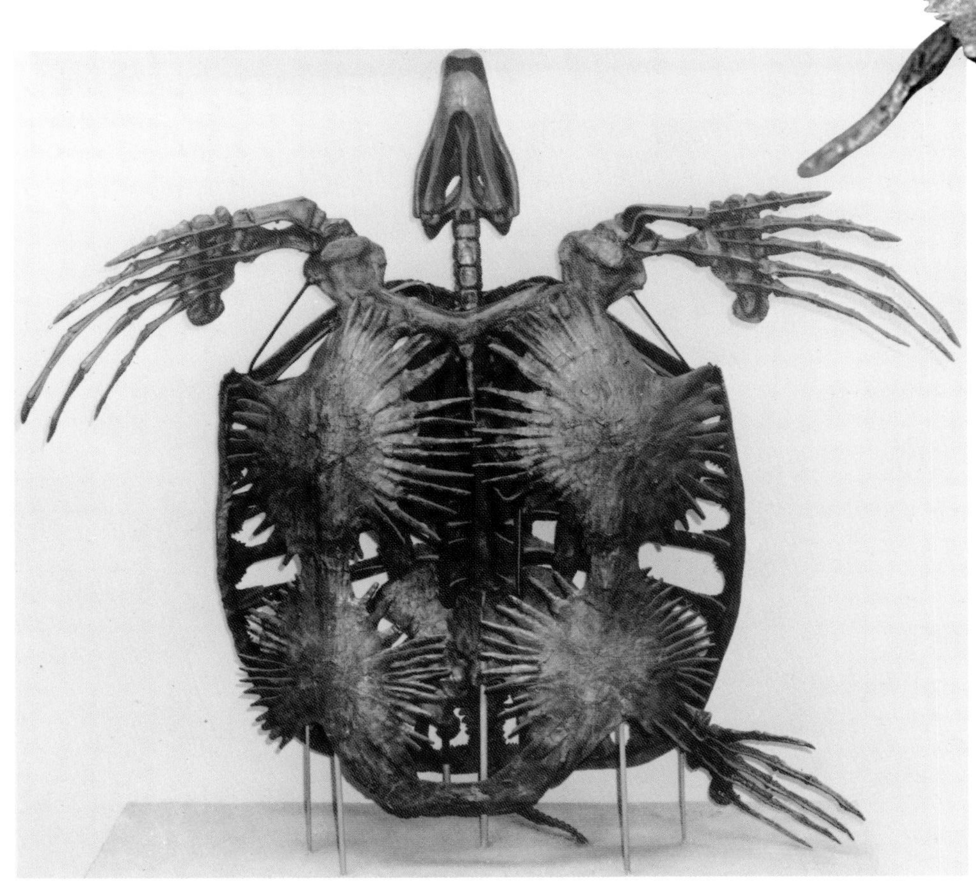

◀ *This skeleton belonged to the giant prehistoric turtle* Archelon. *This monster probably weighed 1.8 tons. It swam in a sea that covered what is now South Dakota 80 million years ago. A bit earlier, large sea turtles also swam in seas over what is now Queensland, Australia.*

vanishing dinosaurs

THE LAST DINOSAURS

At least a dozen kinds of dinosaur still lived in what is now North America just before the mass extinctions at the end of the Cretaceous period. Three of these were the largest ever of their kind: the huge hunter *Tyrannosaurus*, the mighty horned dinosaur *Triceratops*, and the armored dinosaur *Ankylosaurus*. These dinosaurs shared their world with several boneheads, large and small ornithopods, and the sauropod *Alamosaurus*.

Dinosaurs were the most successful backboned animals that ever lived on land. They ruled the earth for approximately 150 million years. Man has only lived on earth for about 2 million years. As old kinds of dinosaur died out, new ones developed and took their place. Some 75 million years ago, parts of what is now western North America teemed with duckbilled, horned, and armored dinosaurs. Yet by 66 million years ago, far fewer species remained and there was no sign of dinosaurs anywhere else. When the Cretaceous period closed 65 million years ago, it seems that all the world's dinosaurs had died.

The end could have come in days or taken thousands of years, nobody knows for certain.

The great dinosaur mystery

Why did the dinosaurs die out? One theory has it that flesh-eating dinosaurs ate all the plant-eating dinosaurs and then starved to death. This had not occurred before, however. A second theory suggests that some dinosaurs were built too awkwardly to walk. A third bright idea is that dinosaurs suffered from some kind of illness or disease that stopped them laying fertile eggs. A fourth explanation is that dinosaurs with thick, spiky skulls or heavy armor had become too strangely shaped and could not adapt to the changes in their surroundings.

Scientists now know that these theories are absurd. Dinosaurs were built in ways that *helped* them to survive.

▼ *Small prehistoric mammals that fed on dinosaur eggs were once thought to have caused the extinction of these mighty creatures. Few people accept this idea today, however, as mammals had lived alongside the dinosaurs for millions of years without posing a threat to them before.*

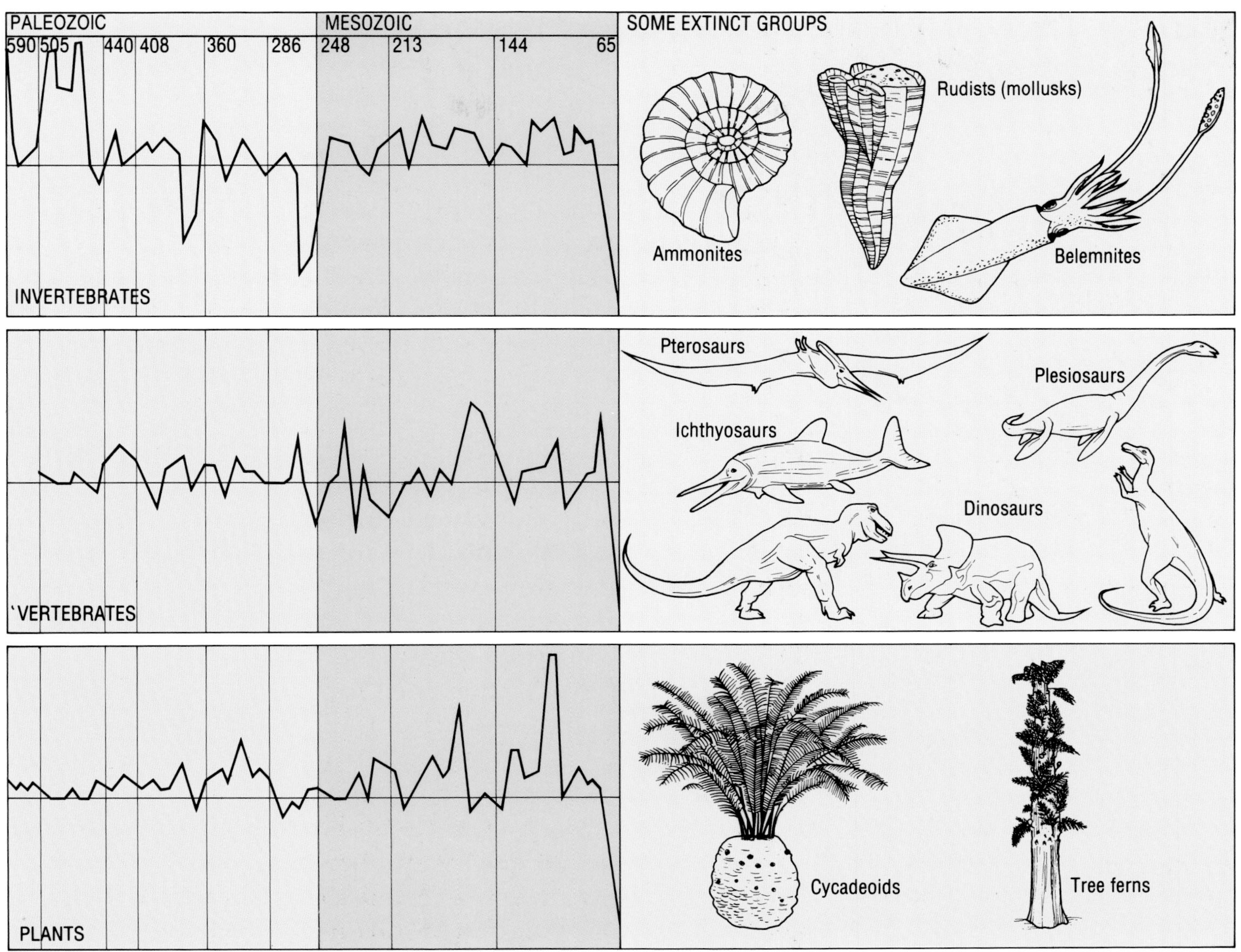

▲ Lines on this graph show the rise and fall in numbers of species of invertebrates, vertebrates, and plants through the Paleozoic and Mesozoic eras. Sharp falls at the end of the Age of Dinosaurs affected all three groups. The three sea creatures at the top were among the many animals without a backbone to become extinct. Vertebrates that vanished included, first, the ichthyosaurs and then the pterosaurs, plesiosaurs, and dinosaurs. The Cretaceous period also saw old kinds of plants such as the cycadeoids die out as flowering shrubs and trees began to take their place.

Killed by enemies?

Several theories blame external enemies for wiping out the dinosaurs. For instance, maybe small mammals ate all their eggs. It is quite likely that mammals did eat some, as lizards eat Nile crocodiles' eggs today. But egg thieves have not killed off all the Nile crocodiles.

Perhaps the dinosaurs were poisoned. Many of the flowering plants that spread over the earth in Late Cretaceous times had poisonous and bitter-flavored leaves. Poisons are plant defenses against being eaten. But poisonous plants first appeared long before the dinosaurs became extinct and dinosaurs knew to avoid them, just as living leaf-eaters do. Anyway, many flowering plants were good to eat. Indeed, horned dinosaurs probably developed their sharp beaks specially to crop these new kinds of tough-leaved flowering plants.

A third possibility is that tiny, invisible enemies destroyed the dinosaurs. Germs passed from beast to beast perhaps spread diseases that killed the dinosaurs. It is very unlikely, however, that such diseases could have killed all the dinosaurs throughout the world.

▲ *Clouds of dust and gas from volcanic eruptions may have destroyed the dinosaurs.*

▼ *An asteroid measuring 6 miles across hurtles down toward the earth (1). The force of the impact would have been more than that of many nuclear bombs (2). Dust and water hurled into the atmosphere would have blotted out the sun for months or years (3). As the temperature dropped, many animals may have died.*

Natural disasters

None of these theories explains why so many other animals died out at the same time as the dinosaurs. All land animals heavier than an eight-year-old child suddenly disappeared. The great pterosaurs became extinct, as did the swimming reptiles the plesiosaurs, and mosasaurs. Hordes of small sea animals without a backbone, such as the ammonites, disappeared too. The reason for these mass deaths must have been some disaster that affected land, sea, and air everywhere.

First, however, came slowly damaging climatic changes. By Late Cretaceous times, sea levels had fallen, slabs of the earth's crust colliding together had pushed up huge new mountain ranges, and big land areas had drifted from the warm tropics into colder regions of the world. All these changes brought cold winters to places that had long been warm and moist. Oaks and other trees that shed their leaves in winter replaced evergreen ferns and cycadeoids. Leaf-eating dinosaurs now faced long, hungry, winter months. Perhaps a lack of winter food explains why some of the last dinosaurs laid thin-shelled eggs that lacked enough calcium to build skeletons for the babies inside.

Asteroid or volcano?

For many Mesozoic animals asteroids raining in from space may have proved the last straw. An asteroid, or several asteroids, each as big as a city, whizzing down at speed would have punched huge holes in the earth's crust and hurled dust and water vapor high into the sky. The sun would have been blotted out for months and all around the world there would have been darkness, freezing cold, and stormy weather. As the

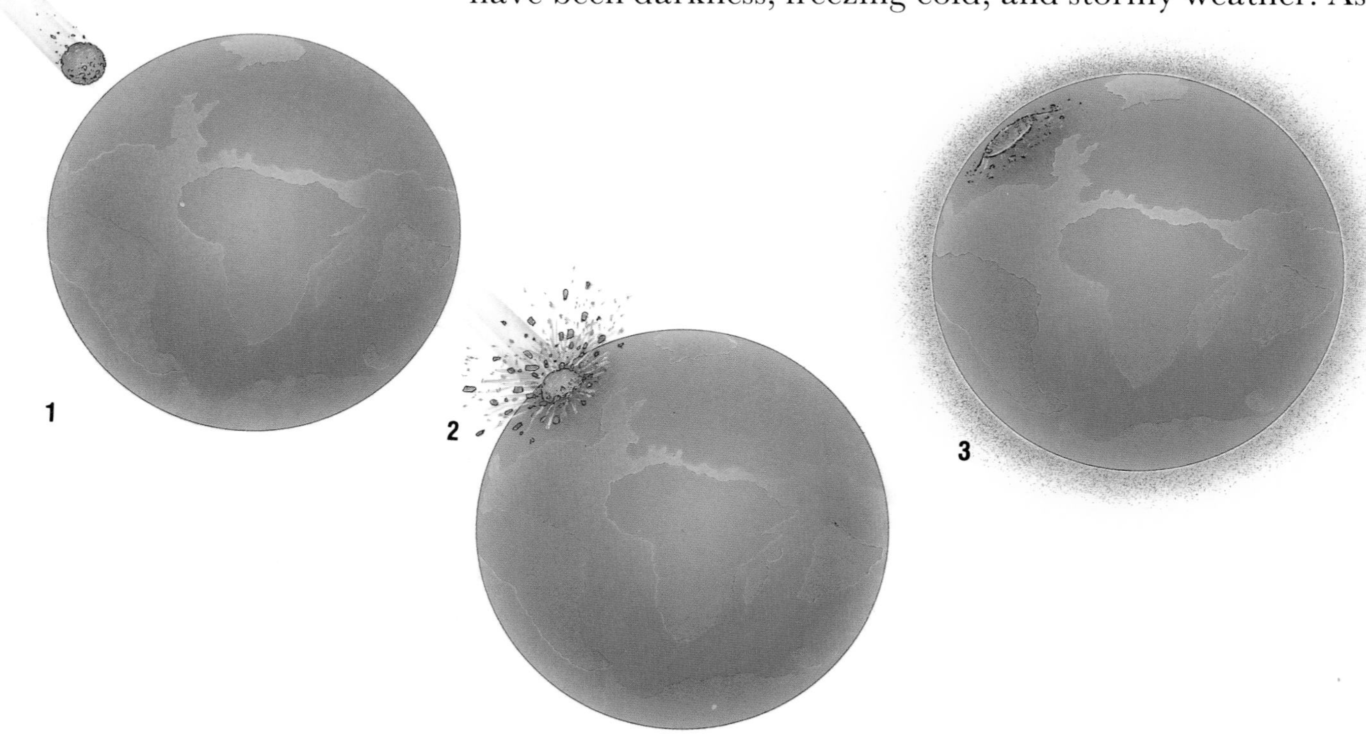

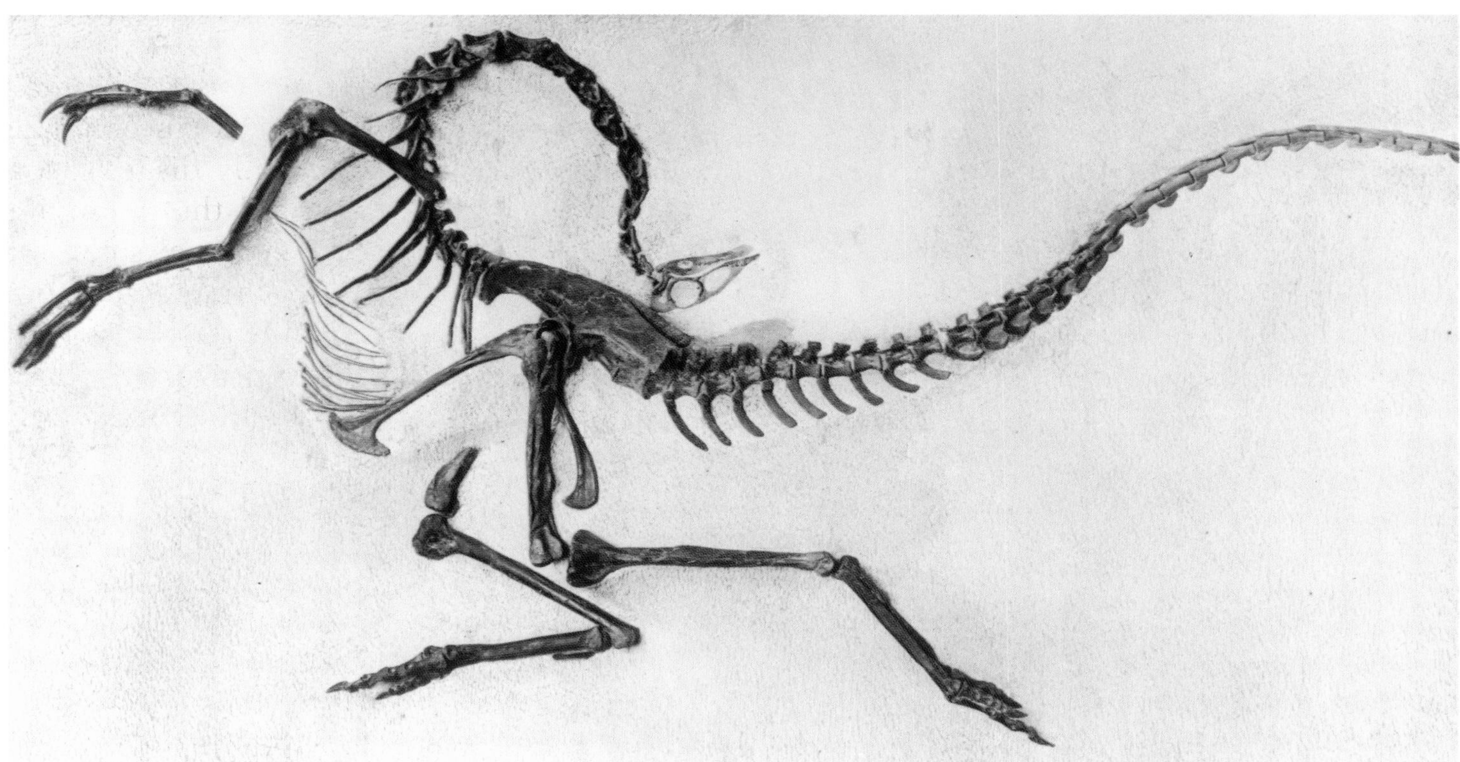

dust settled, water vapor still up in the sky would have trapped the sun's heat near the ground. For a while the world would then have become extremely hot.

Unusual minerals, which could have come from asteroids, have been found in the same rock layer all around the world. These discoveries hint that a shower of asteroids may indeed have hit the earth. But volcanic eruptions could also have produced similar minerals and effects upon the weather. Scientists know that huge volcanic eruptions were going on in India 65 million years ago. Either asteroids or volcanoes could have been responsible for the end of the dinosaurs.

As the world grew dark and cold, small, cold-blooded animals probably burrowed into the ground to hibernate. Warm-blooded birds and mammals could stay active, protected from the cold by their fur or feathers. Most dinosaurs, however, were too big to burrow and, even if they were warm-blooded, they had no fur or feathers to keep them warm. They would have grown numb with cold and died. It is possible that dinosaurs small enough to hibernate survived and laid eggs. However, the unusually hot or cold weather could have affected the sex of the babies in the eggs. As a result, the hatchlings may have been all males or all females. Without females to lay eggs or males to fertilize them there would have been no more baby dinosaurs to replace the old dinosaurs that died.

Nobody knows for sure why the dinosaurs died out, but once they were all dead, birds and mammals quickly multiplied and took their place. If birds really are feathered theropods, however, then the dinosaurs did not become totally extinct and their descendants still share our world today!

▲ *Fossils of dinosaurs with their necks thrown back led some scientists to think that the dinosaurs died of poisoning. But ligaments in the neck that shrink after an animal has died cause the same effect.*

MAMMALS TAKE OVER

The world must have seemed a very empty place after the dinosaurs died out. There were hardly any large land animals left on the earth. The animals that survived the mass extinctions included the birds, lizards, crocodiles and turtles, and small creatures that were covered in fur. These were the mammals. The mammals first appeared in Triassic times, but they had always been overshadowed by the dinosaurs. When these massive animals died out, the mammals soon multiplied to take their place.

dinosaur groups

Triassic
Jurassic
Cretaceous

ankylosauria

This ornithischian suborder contained four-legged plant-eaters there were protected by bony armor in the skin. There were two families: the nodosaurids tended to have narrow heads and long, bony spines jutting out from their sides, while the ankylosaurids had broad heads and a bony tail club. The ankylosaurs appeared in Middle Jurassic times. Most of them lived in northern continents in Late Cretaceous times.

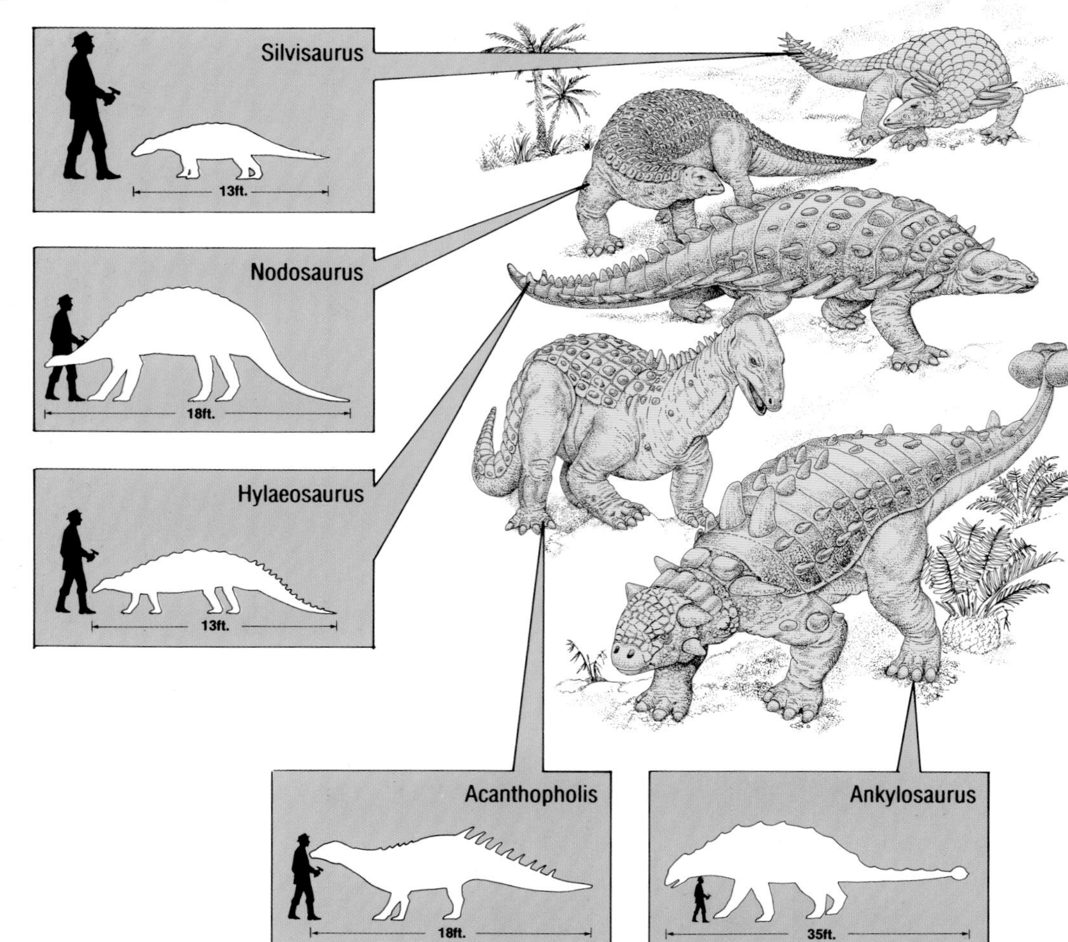

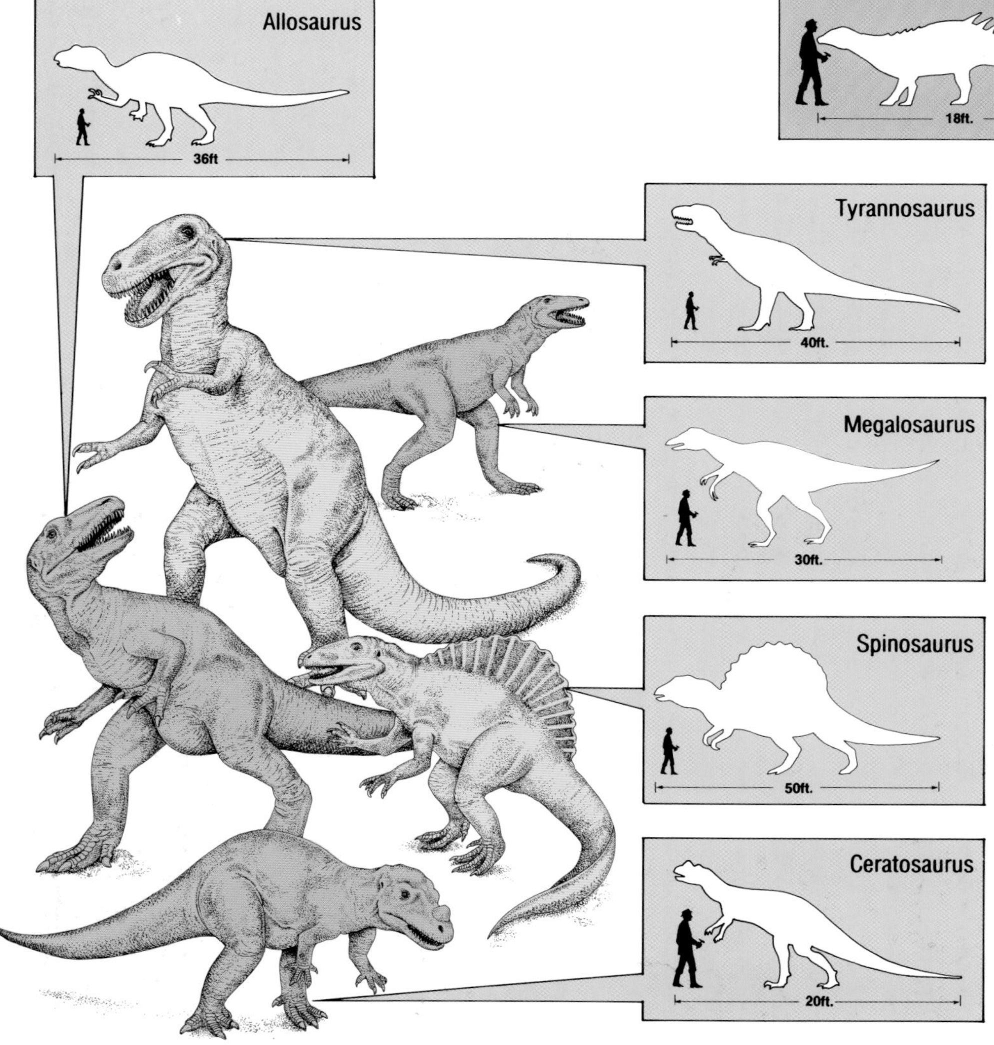

carnosauria

This was an infraorder of the flesh-eating saurischian dinosaurs called theropods. Carnosaurs were large, two-legged dinosaurs with short arms, but huge heads and jaws lined with long, sharp teeth. They may have hunted in packs to kill big plant-eating dinosaurs. The two best known carnosaur families are the allosaurids and the tyrannosaurids. Tyrannosaurids grew up to 40 ft. long and weighed up to 6.4 tons. Some were the largest meat-eaters that ever lived on land. Carnosaurs lived from Early Jurassic to Late Cretaceous times. They spread right across the world.

ceratopsia

The ornithischian suborder Ceratopsia included big horned dinosaurs of the ceratopsid family. These four-legged plant-eaters had a deep beak, a huge, horned head and a broad, bony frill that shielded the back of the neck. Ceratopsids grew from 6 to 30 feet long and lived in Late Cretaceous North America. They were descended from smaller, more primitive ceratopsians that had short frills and bony bumps instead of horns. Such creatures included the protoceratopsids and the two-legged psittacosaurids. Both lived in what is now East Asia.

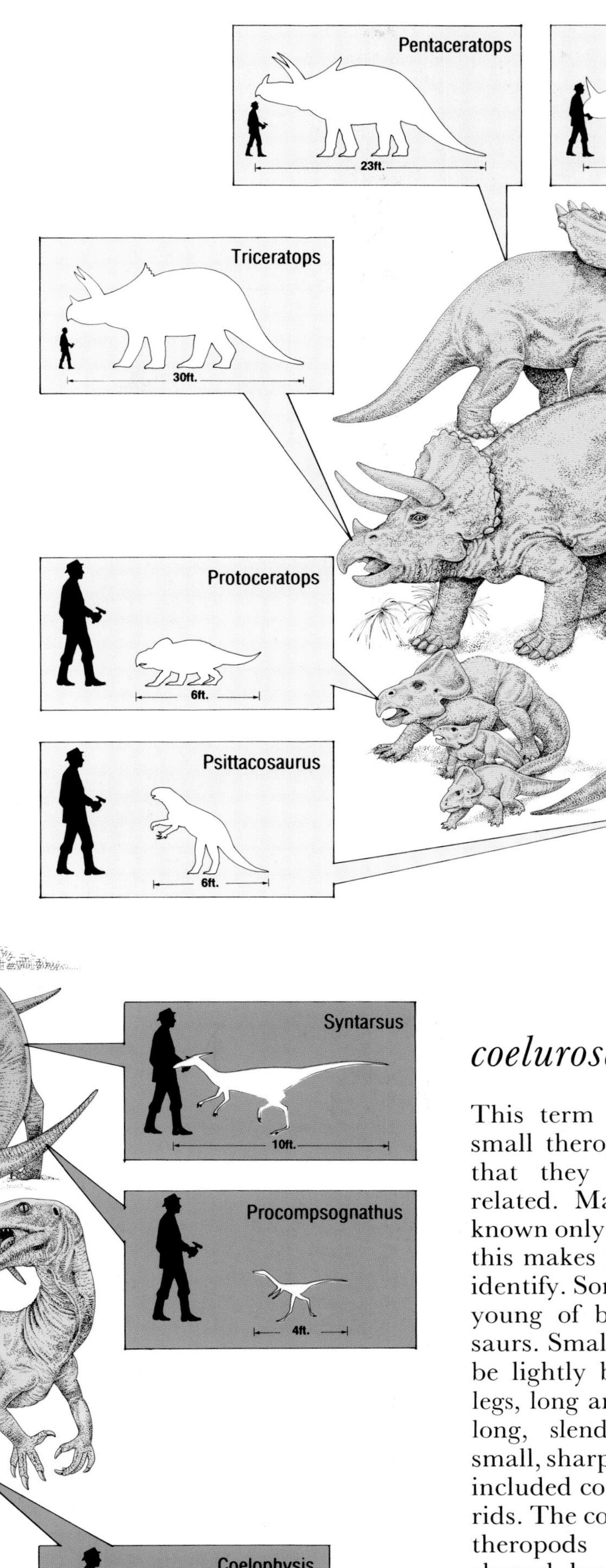

coelurosauria

This term covers a mixture of small theropods. We now know that they were not all truly related. Many coelurosaurs are known only from a few bones and this makes them very difficult to identify. Some may have been the young of big flesh-eating dinosaurs. Small theropods tended to be lightly built. They had long legs, long arms, sharp claws, and long, slender jaws lined with small, sharp teeth. Such creatures included coelophysids and coelurids. The coelophysids were early theropods with big, wedge-shaped heads, and hands with three or four claws. Coelurids came later and had low heads and three-clawed hands. Small theropods lived all over the world.

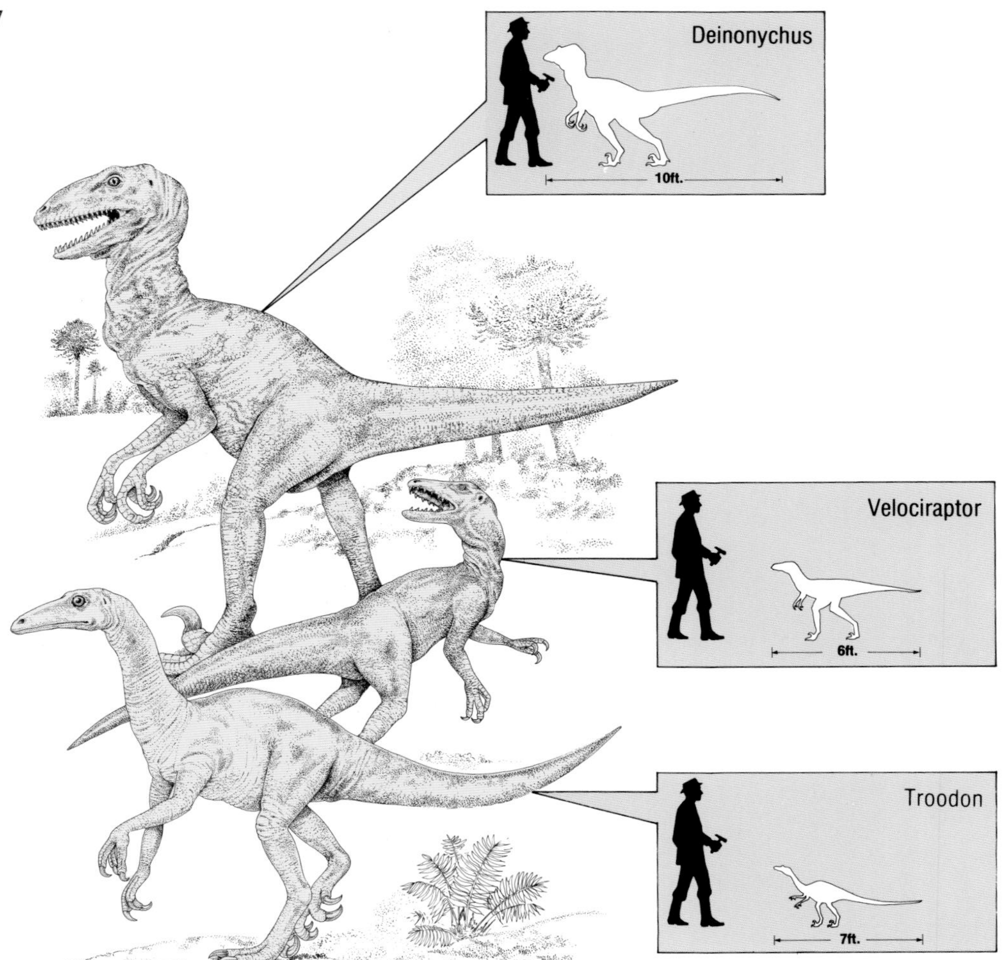

deinonychosauria

This theropod infraorder of lightweight flesh-eaters probably included some of the fiercest and most dangerous of dinosaurs. They may have hunted in packs, sprinting and leaping after their prey on strong, hind limbs. Once they had caught their victim, a long, curved claw on the second toe flicked forward to inflict a slashing wound. There were two families of deinonychosaurs. The dromaeosaurids included the two medium-sized killers *Deinonychus* and *Velociraptor*. *Troodon* and other troodontids were more lightly built than the dromaeosaurids and had a smaller second toe claw. *Troodon* had keen eyes, and its brain was bigger, for its size, than any other dinosaur's. Deinonychosaurs lived in Cretaceous North America and Asia.

ornithomimosauria

This theropod infraorder was made up of a group of advanced running dinosaurs. It included the ornithomimid family of dinosaurs, which are also known as ostrich dinosaurs. Like ostriches, *Struthiomimus* and *Ornithomimus* had big, keen eyes, a toothless beak, a long, curved neck, and long legs. But instead of wings, they had arms and three-clawed hands. They probably fed on plants and small animals. *Elaphrosaurus* lived in Late Jurassic Africa, but most other ornithomimids came from Late Cretaceous North America and East Asia. The strange, short-headed oviraptorids such as *Oviraptor* looked a bit like ostrich dinosaurs, but they belong in their own infraorder: oviraptorosauria.

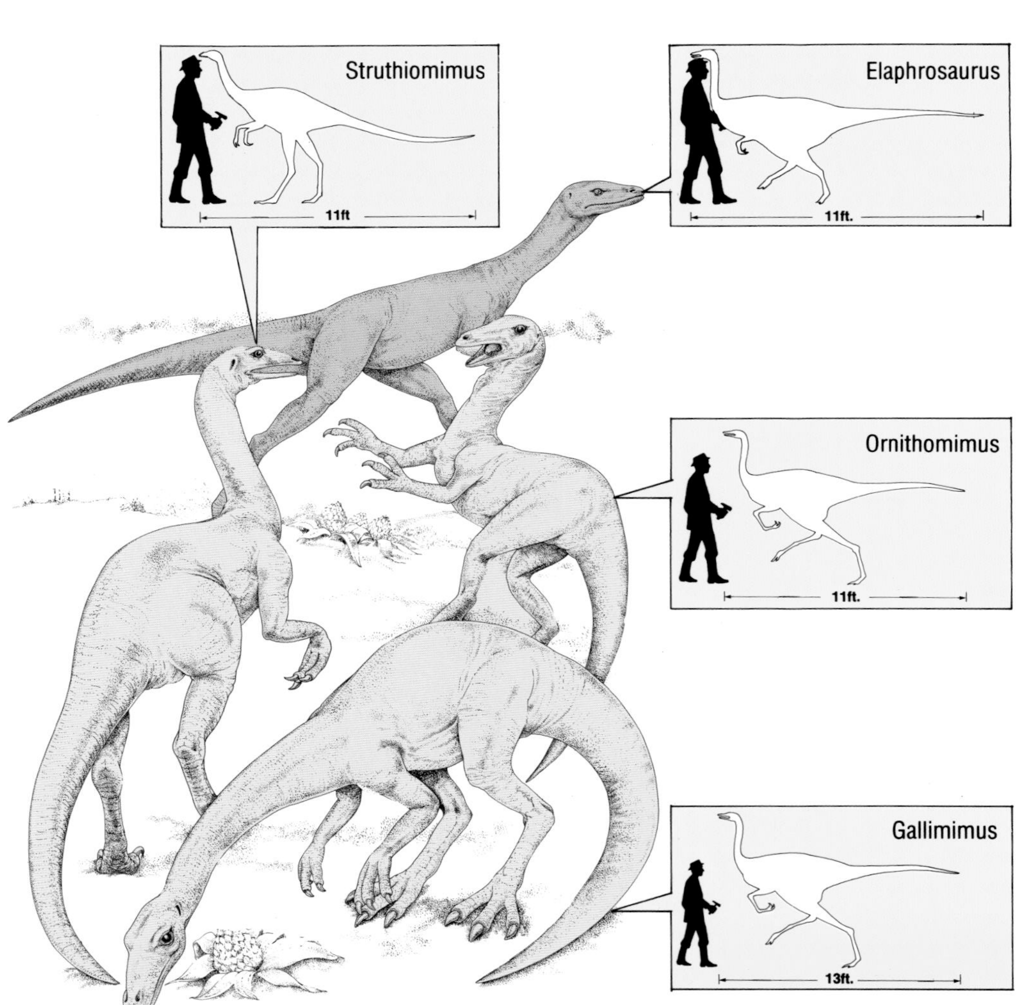

ornithopoda

Ornithopods, or "bird-footed" ornithischians, were a suborder of plant-eaters that lived all through the Age of Dinosaurs and spread right across the world. Some ornithopods looked rather like theropods, as many walked and ran on their hind limbs. But instead of sharp fangs, they had leaf-shaped teeth, horny beaks and cheeks. Small ornithopods, such as the heterodontosaurids and the hypsilophodontids, gave rise to larger ornithopods, including *Camptosaurus* and *Iguanodon*. The largest of all the ornithopods were the Late Cretaceous hadrosaurids, also known as duckbilled dinosaurs. These grew up to 50ft. long and may have weighed as much as 16 tons. They included *Edmontosaurus* and *Parasaurolophus*, both of which lived in what is now North America.

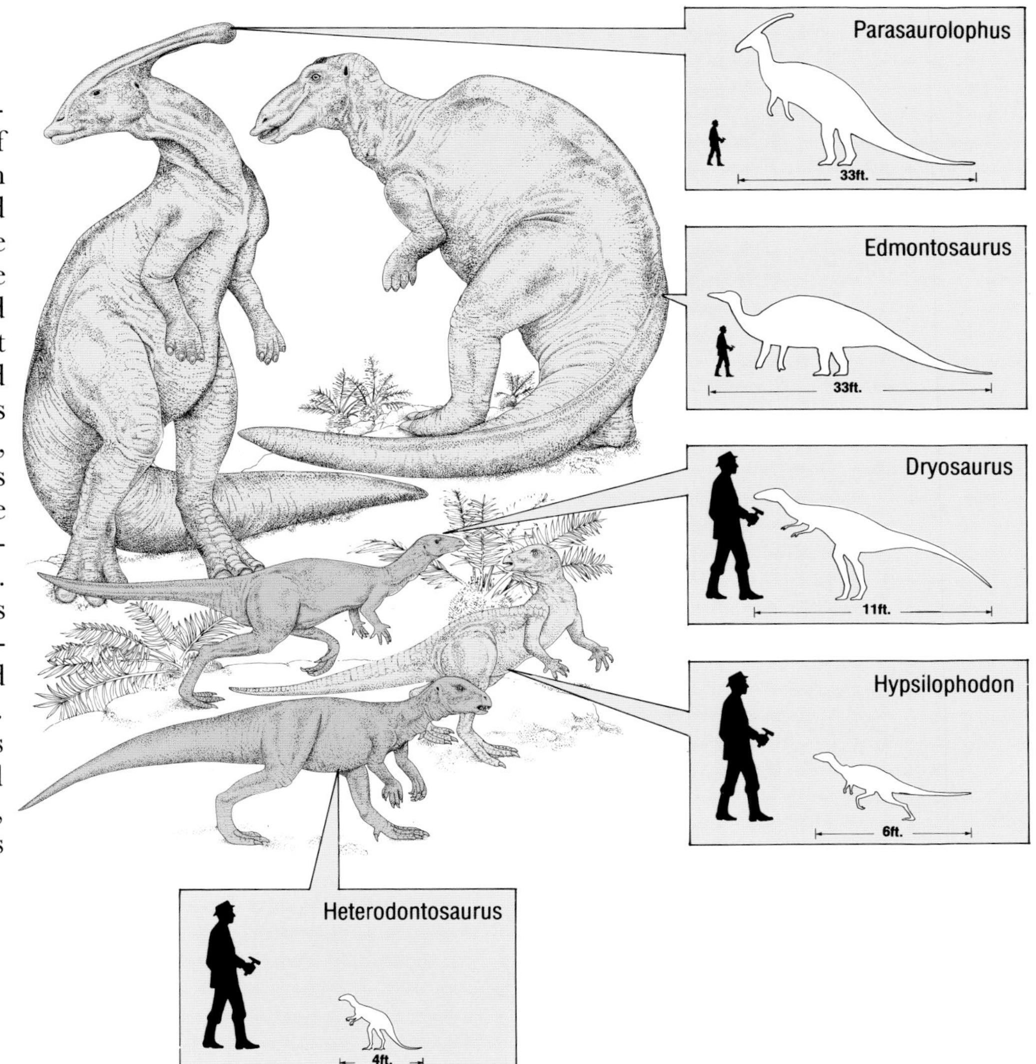

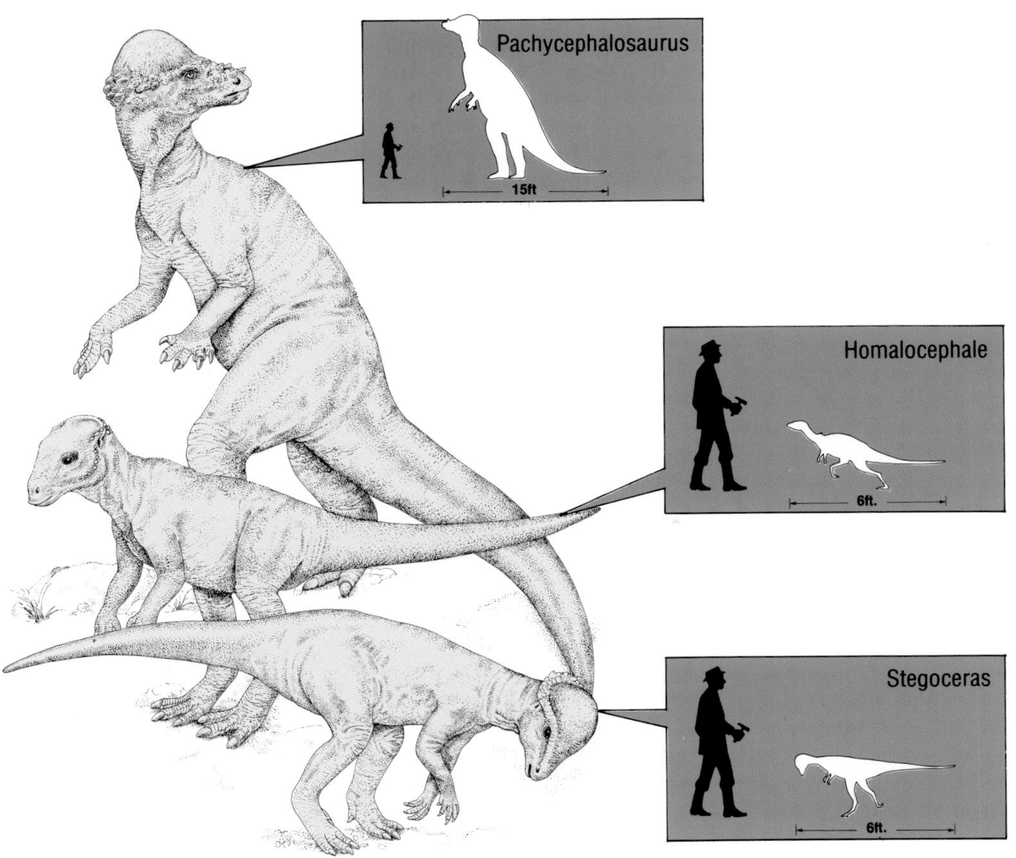

pachycephalosauria

These two-legged plant-eaters made up their own suborder among ornithischians. Their most unusual feature was a thick skull roof that protected the brain, rather like a crash helmet. Scientists suggest that male pachycephalosaurs used to crack heads together to decide who should rule a herd of females. Some scientists split the pachycephalosaurs into two families. One included flat-headed beasts such as *Homalocephale* from present-day Mongolia, the other included dome-headed dinosaurs such as *Pachycephalosaurus* and *Stegoceras*. These lived in what is now North America. Most pachycephalosaurs lived in Late Cretaceous times.

prosauropoda

This saurischian infraorder contained medium to large plant-eaters with quite long necks and tails, bulky bodies and small heads. They evolved in Late Triassic times from two-legged ancestors and died out early in Jurassic times. *Anchisaurus*, from present-day North America, was just over 6 feet long, but other prosauropods such as *Plateosaurus* and *Lufengosaurus* grew three times longer than that. Among the largest of all was 40-foot-long *Melanosaurus* that lived in what is now South Africa. Small, early prosauropods walked on their hind limbs; later prosauropods were bigger and heavier and walked on all fours.

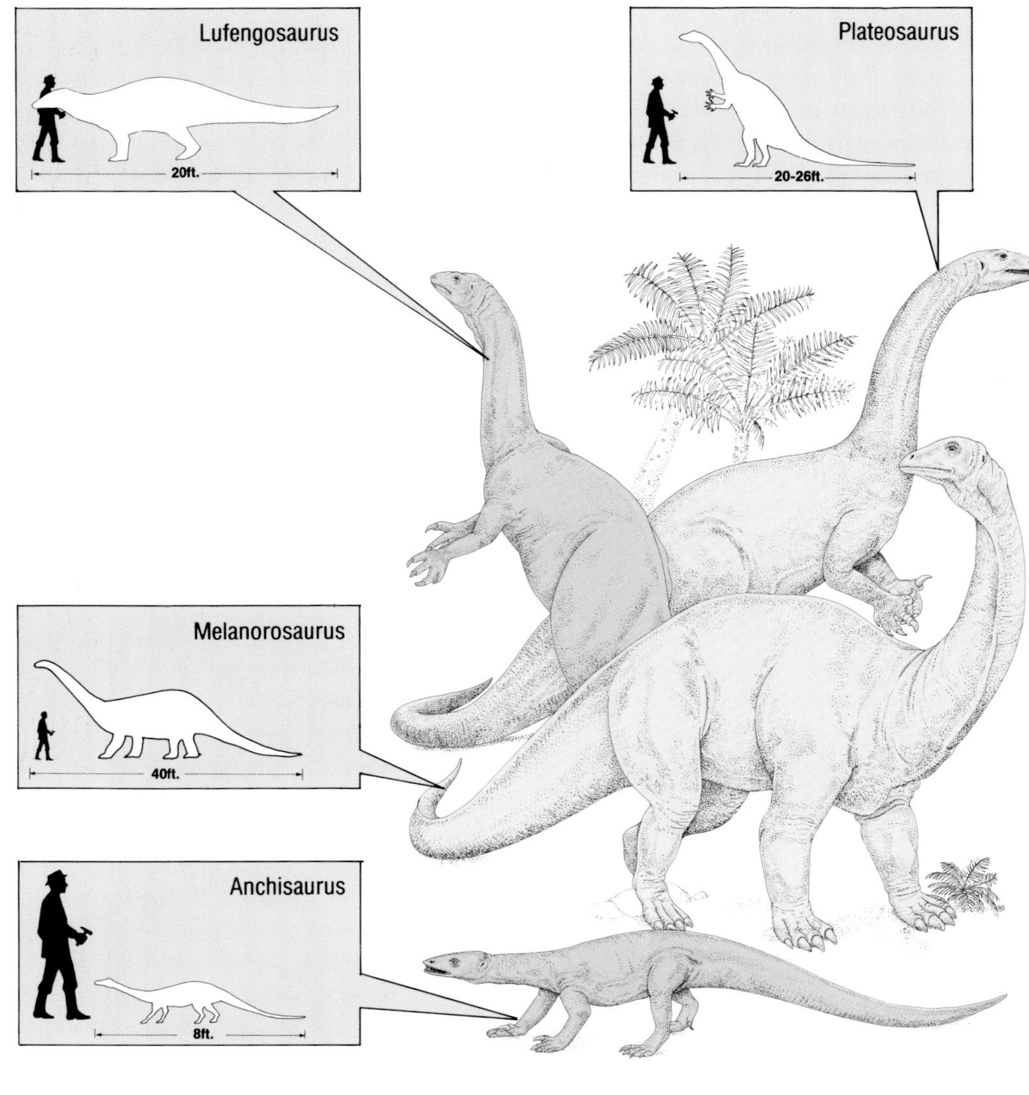

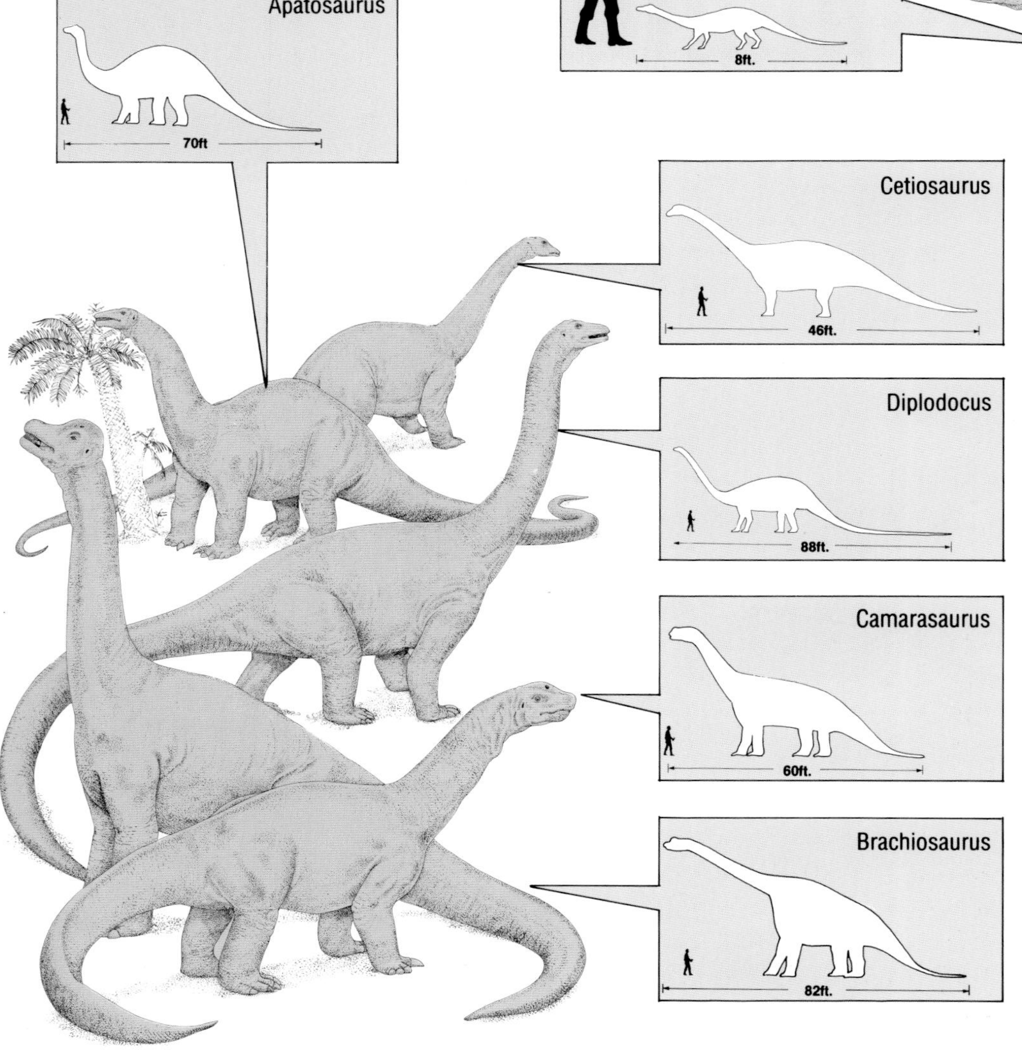

sauropoda

The largest and longest dinosaurs belonged to this saurischian infraorder. Sauropods were huge plant-eaters with long necks and tails, and limbs like tree trunks. They had tiny heads for their size and some of the smallest brains of any backboned animal. The sauropods were descended from the prosauropods. They evolved in the Jurassic period, but most had died out before the end of the Cretaceous. There were several families of sauropods, including the camarasaurids, the cetiosaurids, the diplodocids, and the brachiosaurids. Cetiosaurids included early sauropods. The camarasaurid *Camarasaurus*, the diplodocids *Diplodocus* and *Apatosaurus*, and the brachiosaurid *Brachiosaurus* all lived in Late Jurassic North America.

segnosauria

Segnosaurs were such unusual saurischians that scientists have given them a suborder all to themselves. What makes them so unusual is their hip structure, which is not at all like a typical saurischian "lizard hip." So far, all the segnosaur skeletons that have been recovered have been incomplete, but scientsts think that these curious dinosaurs had light-built bodies, powerful arms, strong legs, and short, broad four-toed feet with long claws. Their narrow heads had cheeks, small, sharp cheek teeth, and a toothless, horny beak. *Segnosaurus*, the largest segnosaur, grew 30 feet long. Scientists are still unsure how these dinosaurs lived. They were probably quite slow-moving creatures and may even have had webbed feet. One possibility is that they swam and hunted fish for food. Some scientists, however, think that this is very unlikely as slippery fish could have wriggled out of a segnosaur's toothless beak very easily. The segnosaurs lived in China and Mongolia during the Late Cretaceous period.

stegosauria

This ornithischian suborder was made up of four-legged plant-eaters that had rows of spikes or bony plates along their backs. The bony spikes would have been used to defend the animals from hungry carnosaurs. The plates may have been used to control the dinosaurs' body temperature. Early Jurassic dinosaurs such as *Scelidosaurus* were probably the ancestors of the stegosaurs and ankylosaurs. True stegosaurs included *Dacentrurus*, *Kentrosaurus*, and *Stegosaurus*. All had bulky bodies and strong limbs. Their small heads contained a brain that was no bigger than a dog's and was often even smaller. Stegosaurs grew from 10 to 30 feet long and lived from Mid Jurassic to Late Cretaceous times.

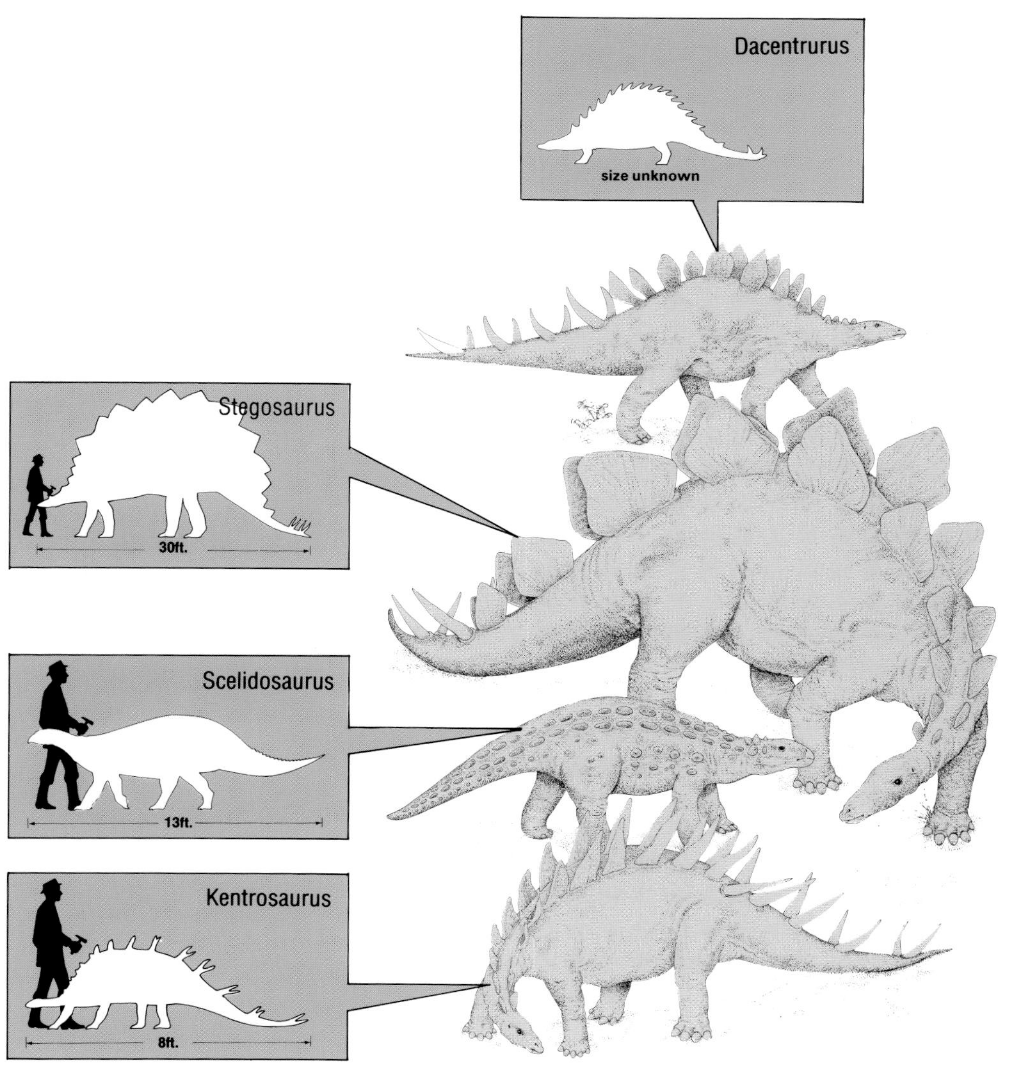

illustrated glossary

► Branchiosaurus, *an early amphibian, lived during the Carboniferous period, some 300 million years ago.*

A

Amino acids Organic compounds that are found in all living things. They join together to form proteins.

Ammonite An extinct mollusk related to the octopus and squid that lived during the Mesozoic era. Ammonites had flat, tightly coiled shells.

Amphibian A moist-skinned animal that can live in both water and air. Frogs, newts, and salamanders are all amphibians. Most amphibians breed and lay their eggs in water. They have gills during the early part of their lives, and can breathe underwater, but the adult animals can leave the water to breathe air.

Archosaurs A group of reptiles that evolved at the end of the Permian period. They eventually, gave rise to the dinosaurs.

Arthropod An invertebrate animal with a jointed body and limbs. Insects, spiders, and lobsters are all arthropods, as were the trilobites.

Atom A tiny particle about 250-millionth of an inch across. Everying is made up of atoms.

B

Belemnite An extinct squidlike mollusk that died out at the end of the Mesozoic era.

Blue-green algae One-celled, plantlike organisms usually found in water. Blue-green algae were probably one of the first living organisms to evolve on earth.

Brachiopod A shelled animal that was common in prehistoric seas, but is much rarer today. Brachiopods have two shells of different shapes.

C

Cambrian period A period of geological time that lasted from 590 to 505 million years ago. It is the first period of the Paleozoic era. During the Cambrian period a wide variety of complex living things evolved, but none of them had backbones.

Carboniferous period The fifth period of the Paleozoic era. It lasted from 360 to 286 million years ago and gets its name from the seams of coal (carbon) that formed from the remains of plants that lived at this time.

Cells The basic units that make up all living things. Some simple organisms are made up of only one cell, but there are millions of cells in a human body.

Cenozoic era A major division of geological time. It is also known as the Age of Recent Life. It extends from the end of the Mesozoic era, 65 million years ago, to the present day. During the Cenozoic era many new kinds of mammal appeared, including the first human beings.

Cold-blooded An animal that is cold-blooded cannot control its own body temperature and relies on the heat of the sun to keep it warm. Amphibians, reptiles, and fish are all cold-blooded animals.

Cretaceous period The third period of the Mesozoic era. It lasted from 144 to 65 million years ago. During this time the dinosaurs continued to dominate the land. At the end of the Cretaceous, however, the dinosaurs disappeared.

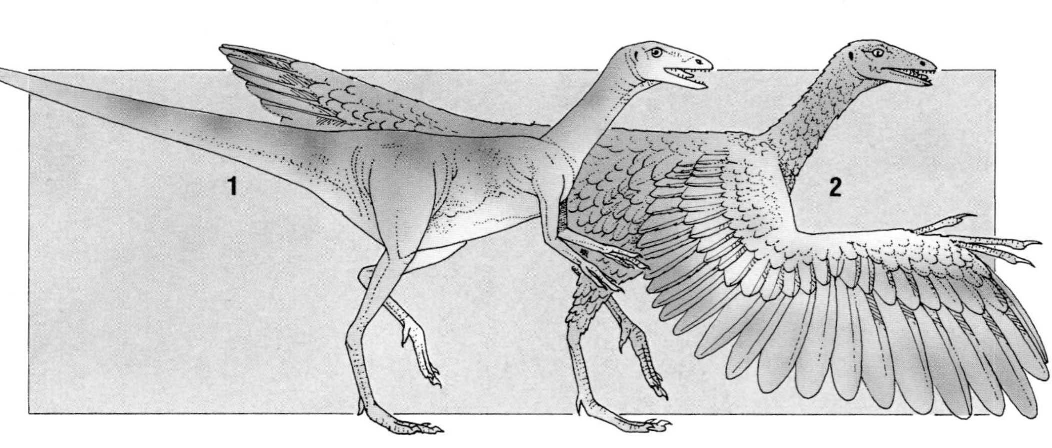

► *Fossils of the dinosaur* Compsognathus *and the early bird* Archaeopteryx *look very similar and have sometimes been confused. Scientists now think that the birds may have developed from small, lightweight theropods such as* Compsognathus.

D

Devonian period The fourth period of the Paleozoic era. It lasted from 408 to 360 million years ago. Many kinds of fish lived during this period. Amphibians also evolved and moved on to the land.

Dicynodonts A group of plant-eating mammal-like reptiles that evolved early in the Permian period.

Dinosaur A term meaning "terrible reptile" used to refer to any of a group of extinct meat-eating or plant-eating reptiles that dominated life on earth from 230 to 65 million years ago.

E-F

Era A major division of time used in geology. There are three eras in the history of the earth and each is divided into a number of periods.

Fossil The remains of an animal or plant that have been preserved in rock.

G

Geologist A scientist who studies the origin, history, and structure of the earth.

Gondwana The land mass that made up the southern part of the supercontinent Pangaea in Triassic times. It included present-day Africa, South America, India, Australia, and Antarctica.

I-J

Ichthyosaurs A group of marine reptiles that looked very like modern dolphins. Ichthyosaurs appeared in the Late Triassic period and survived until the Late Cretaceous period. They reached a length of 33 feet and were powerful swimmers.

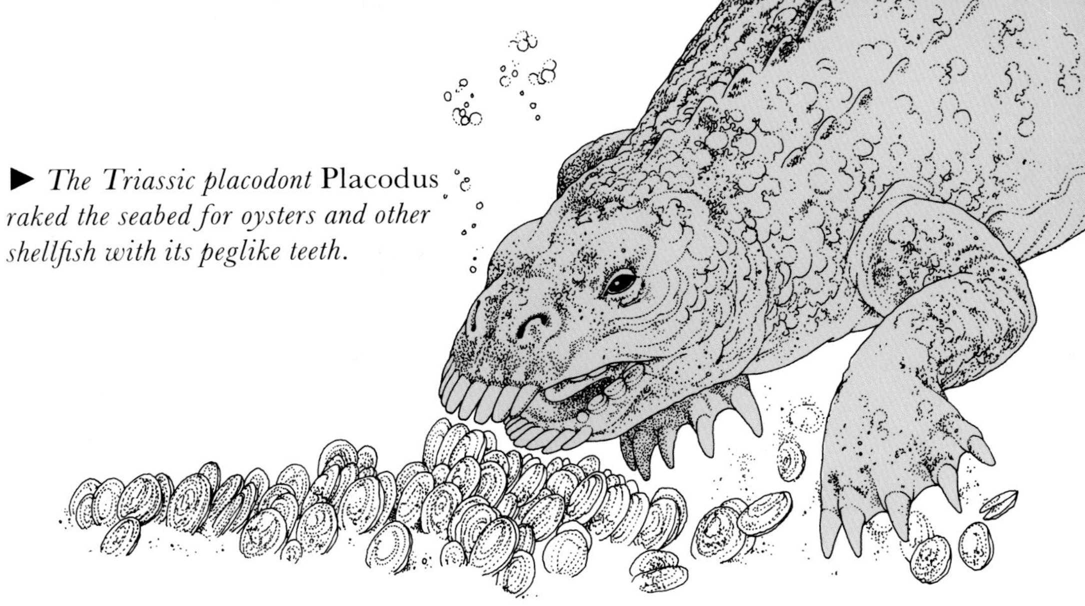

▶ *The Triassic placodont* Placodus *raked the seabed for oysters and other shellfish with its peglike teeth.*

Invertebrate An animal that does not have a backbone. Sponges, jellyfish, worms, shellfish, insects, spiders, and crabs are all invertebrates.

Jurassic period The second of the three periods of the Mesozoic era. During this period, which lasted from 213 to 144 million years ago, dinosaurs ruled on land and the first birds appeared.

K-L

Labyrinthodonts An early group of amphibians. Some were tiny, others grew as large as crocodiles. From these large labyrinthodonts came the reptiles.

Laurasia The major land mass that made up the northern part of the supercontinent Pangaea in Triassic times. It included present-day Europe, Asia, and North America.

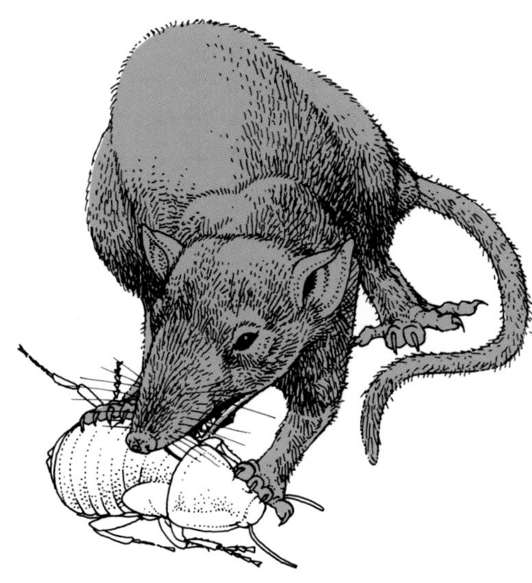

▶ Morganucodon *was an early mammal that lived in Triassic times. Later mammals have been blamed for the extinction of the dinosaurs.*

Lepospondyls A group of primitive amphibians that lived in Carboniferous times. Some spent all their lives in water, others had strong limbs and spent most of their time on dry land. Modern amphibians are descended from this second group.

Lobe-finned fish A group of fish with fleshy fins that are closely related to the amphibians. The lobe-fins were the first land-living vertebrates.

M

Mammal A warm-blooded animal that feeds its young with milk. Mammals are usually more or less covered by fur or hair. Mice, dogs, horses, elephants, and humans are all mammals.

Mammal-like reptiles A group of reptiles that dominated the land at the beginning of the Permian period. They eventually gave rise to the mammals.

Mesozoic era A major division of geological time. It lasted from 248 to 65 million years ago and is also known as the Age of Dinosaurs. The Mesozoic is divided into the Triassic, the Jurassic, and the Cretaceous periods.

Molecule A chemical unit made up of two or more atoms that have joined together.

Mollusk A soft-bodied invertebrate, usually with a hard protective shell. Mollusks include animals such as snails, mussels, cuttlefish, slugs, the octopus, and the extinct ammonites and belemnites.

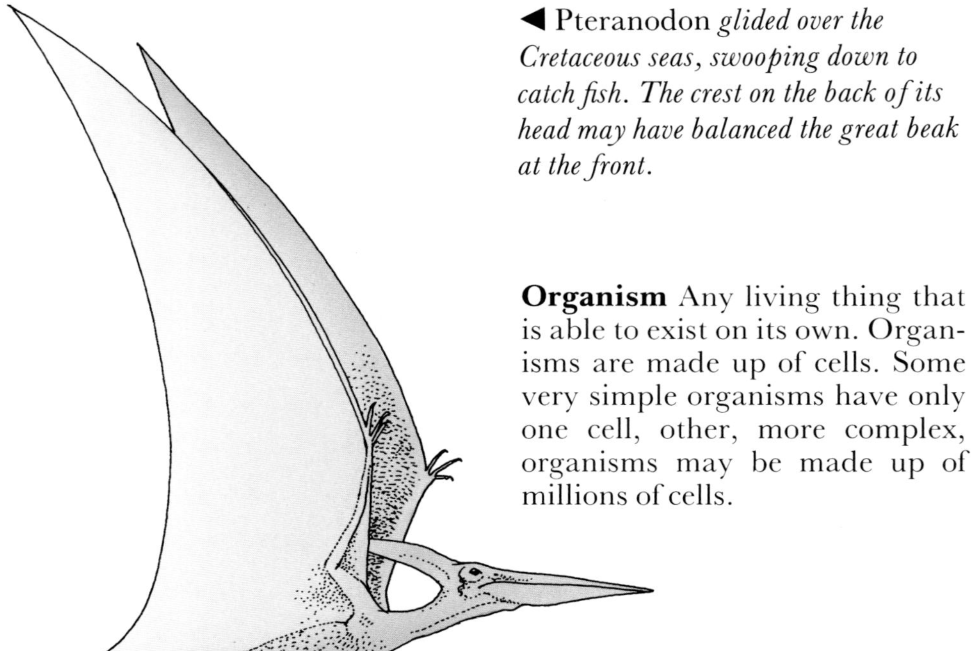

◀ Pteranodon *glided over the Cretaceous seas, swooping down to catch fish. The crest on the back of its head may have balanced the great beak at the front.*

Mosasaurs Giant seagoing lizards, measuring up to 50 feet long, that lived in the Late Cretaceous period.

N-O

Nautiloid A mollusk with a coiled shell related to the ammonites. Nautiloids have lived from the Devonian period to the present day.
Nothosaurs A group of marine reptiles that lived in Triassic times. They ranged from 15 inches to 20 feet in length.
Nucleic acids Complex molecules found in the cells of all living things. They control the development of the cell.
Ordovician period The second period of the Paleozoic era. It lasted from 505 to 440 million years ago. During the Ordovician period the first coral reefs were formed, new groups of mollusks evolved and the first vertebrates appeared.

Organism Any living thing that is able to exist on its own. Organisms are made up of cells. Some very simple organisms have only one cell, other, more complex, organisms may be made up of millions of cells.

Ornithischian A term used to describe one of the two main groups of dinosaurs. Ornithischian means "bird-hipped" and refers to the shape of the hip area. Ornithischian dinosaurs were all plant-eaters.

P

Paleontologist A scientist who studies fossils of prehistoric plants and animals in order to work out how the earth and life on it evolved.
Paleozoic era A major division of geological time also known as the Age of Ancient Life. It lasted from 590 to 248 million years ago and is divided into six periods: the Cambrian, Ordovician, Silurian, Devonian, Carboniferous, and Permian periods.
Pangaea The giant supercontinent that was made up of all the land masses of the earth before the start of the Mesozoic era.
Pelycosaurs A group of early mammal-like reptiles that lived in the Permian period. Most pelycosaurs had a skin "sail" on their backs that acted as a heat radiator.
Period In geological time, a subdivision of an era. The dinosarus evolved in the Triassic period and died out in the Cretaceous period – all in the Mesozoic era.
Permian period The geological period that ended the Paleozoic era. During this period, which lasted from 286 to 248 million years ago, the reptiles spread rapidly.
Photosynthesis A chemical process in which plants combine water and carbon dioxide from the air to make food. It depends on the presence of a green pigment called chlorophyll and relies on the energy of sunlight. One of the products of this chemical process is oxygen.
Placodonts A group of marine reptiles that lived in the Triassic seas. They grew between 6 and 10 feet long and fed on shellfish.
Plesiosaurs A group of long-necked, flat-bellied marine reptiles that lived during the Jurassic and Cretaceous periods. They reached a length of over 40 feet.
Pliosaurs A group of large, ferocious, short-necked plesiosaurs that lived in the sea during the Cretaceous period. They fed on other marine creatures.
Precambrian era A major division of geological time. It lasted some 4 billion years, from the birth of the earth to the start of the Paleozoic era.
Protein Any of a large number of complex molecules made up of nucleic acids. Proteins are essen-

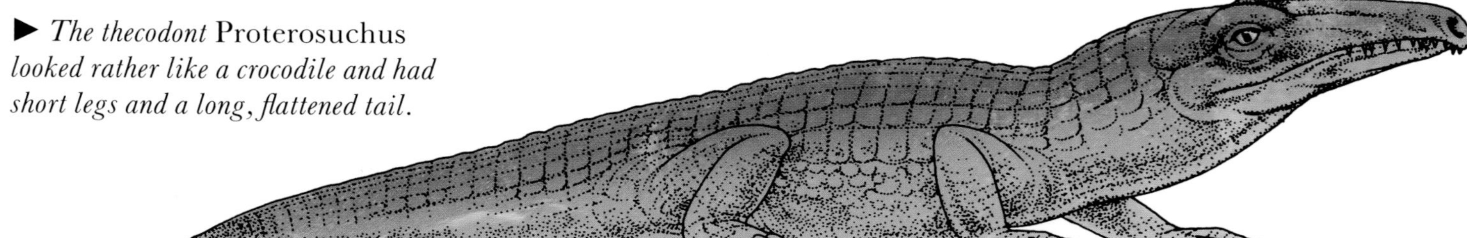

► *The thecodont* Proterosuchus *looked rather like a crocodile and had short legs and a long, flattened tail.*

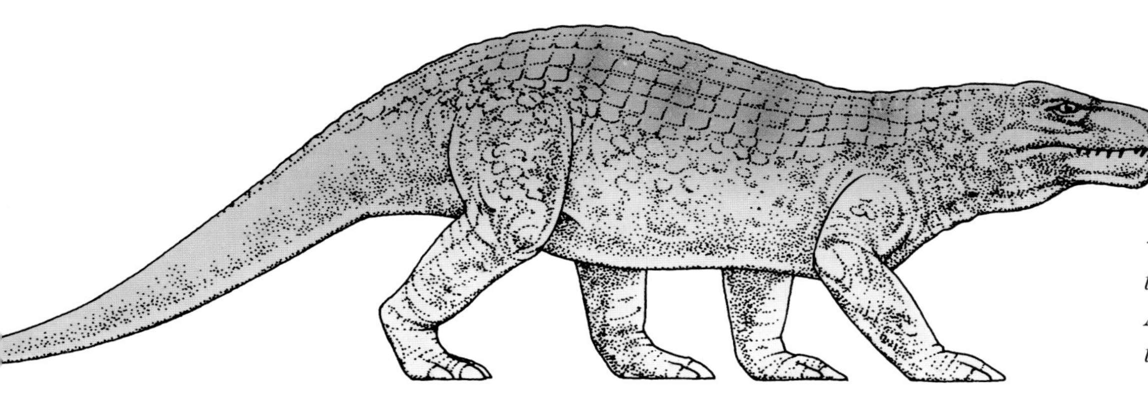

◀ Shansisuchus, *an early thecodont, lived in Triassic times. Animals such as these were to lead to the dinosaurs.*

tial to life, as they make up most of the tissues of all living organisms.

Pterodactyloids A group of pterosaurs that lived in the Cretaceous period. Some of them were much larger than the earlier pterosaurs, the rhamphorhynchoids.

Pterosaurs A group of Mesozoic winged reptiles related to the dinosaurs and crocodilians. Pterosaurs of the Triassic and Jurassic periods are known as rhamphorhynchoids, while later pterosaurs are called pterodactyloids.

Q-R

Reptile A cold-blooded air-breathing vertebrate covered in scales. Alligators and crocodiles, lizards and turtles are all reptiles.

Rhamphorhynchoids A group of pterosaurs that lived in the Triassic and Jurassic periods. The rhamphorhynchoids had fairly short, broad wings and some had very long tails.

Rhipidistians A group of lobe-finned fish that gave rise to the amphibians. They had lungs and could breathe air. Rhipidistians were common in Devonian times.

Rhynchosaurs A group of reptiles that evolved during the Triassic period and spread across the world. They had beaklike mouths with large teeth.

S

Saurischian The term used to describe one of the two main groups of dinosaurs. Saurischian means "lizard-hipped" and refers to the shape of the hip area. Saurishcian dinosaurs included both plant-eaters and meat-eaters.

Sedimentary rock A kind of rock formed from sediments of fine mud and sand that were deposited in seas and lakes millions of years ago.

Silurian period The third period of the Paleozoic era. During this period, which lasted from 440 to 408 million years ago, the first jawed fish appeared and also the first land plants.

Species A basic group of plants or animals that are all similar and can breed together. Human beings form one species, chimpanzees form another, and so on.

T

Thecodonts An early group of archosaurs that lived in the Triassic period. They included the ancestors of the dinosaurs, the pterosaurs and the crocodilians.

Therapsids A group of mammal-like reptiles that developed at the end of the Permian period. They were descended from the pelycosaurs and eventually gave rise to the mammals.

Theropods A group of flesh-eating dinosaurs including the coelurosaurs and the carnosaurs.

Triassic period The first period of the Mesozoic era. It lasted from 248 to 144 million years ago. During this time the reptiles evolved to produce the first dinosaurs and large marine reptiles.

Trilobite An arthropod with many legs that was common on the seabed between Cambrian and Silurian times. A trilobite's body was divided into three sections and its eyes were made up of many tiny lenses.

V

Vertebrate An animal with a skull and backbone. About 43,000 species of vertebrate are known. Vertebrates include fish, amphibians, reptiles, birds, and mammals.

W

Warm-blooded An animal that can control its own body temperature is called warm-blooded. Warm-blooded animals usually have fur or feathers to help them keep heat in. Birds and mammals are examples of warm-blooded animals.

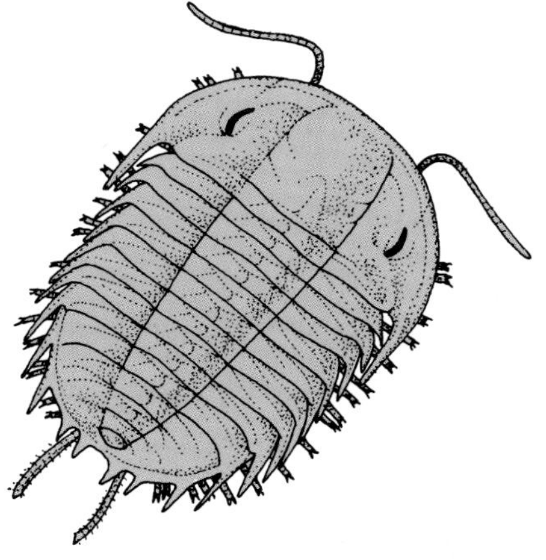

◀ *Trilobites hunted for food on the seabed throughout the Paleozoic era. They could run quite quickly and may also have used their many legs for swimming. Most trilobites had very complex eyes that were made up of many tiny lenses. This meant they could see forward, backward, and sideways at the same time.*

index

Figures in *italics* refer to illustrations

93